GW00566882

"I love everything Joar
Shadow is the icing on t
gold within the darknes
the way."

— Steven Pressfield, author of *The War of Art*

"*Writing the Shadow* is so much more than a book. It's a compilation of self-healing practices, a workbook of soul-searching questions, an annotated reading list, and a generous personal history in which the author reveals her own "dark little heart." Holding our hand, Penn faces fearlessly into shadows of all shapes and colours, and shows how venturing into the heart of darkness is necessary for any writer who wants to shine a light."

— Orna Ross, novelist, poet and founder of the Alliance of Independent Authors

"As someone obsessed with darkness, difference, and the things that lurk between, *Writing the Shadow* is the book I didn't know I needed. It's as insightful as it is empowering. If you're a writer looking to deepen yourself, your business or craft, I dare you to read this and not come out a better person.

I wish this book could be gifted to every new writer so they understand what took me too long to grasp: that stay true to yourself in your work and craft is the fastest path to success."

— Sacha Black/Ruby Roe

"No matter what stage of your writing adventure you're in, this book will be a guide through some of the toughest parts of the journey. Penn's work shines, not just as a great aid to writers, but as a stunningly brave look inside the mind of one of the best writers around."

— Michaelbrent Collings, #1 bestseller and
multiple Bram Stoker Award finalist

"Penn's *Writing the Shadow* is both a call to explore our own hidden depths, and a torch to see by as we do."

— Toby Neal, Creator of the Paradise Crime World

"If you want to go authentically deep into your writing, you must to be brave enough to look into the shadows you bring to the page (whether you mean to or not). With kindness, honesty, and courage, Joanna Penn shows you how to do it in *Writing the Shadow*, a book every writer should keep close at hand."

— Rachael Herron, novelist, memoirist,
and bestselling author of Fast-Draft Your Memoir

"You cannot fulfil your potential as a writer unless you face – and embrace – your Shadow. Joanna Penn is the perfect guide through the darkness, having trodden the path in her own writer's quest. *Writing the Shadow* will light the way to the treasure in your own inner labyrinth."

— Mark McGuinness, Poet and Creative Coach

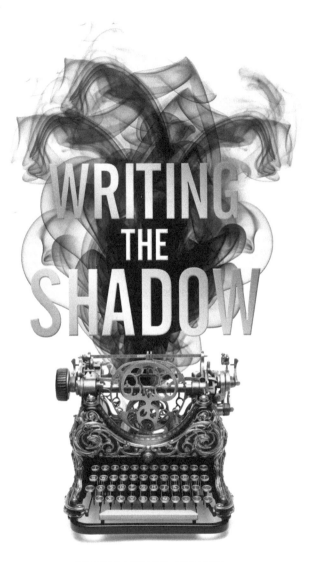

WRITING THE SHADOW

TURN YOUR INNER
DARKNESS INTO WORDS

Joanna Penn

Ebook ISBN: 978-1-915425-08-9
Special Edition Kickstarter Hardback ISBN: 978-1-915425-39-3
Hardback ISBN: 978-1-915425-40-9
Paperback ISBN: 978-1-915425-41-6
Large Print ISBN: 978-1-915425-42-3
Audio ISBN: 978-1-915425-44-7
Workbook ISBN: 978-1-915425-45-4

Published by Curl Up Press

Requests to publish work from this book should be sent to:
joanna@ TheCreativePenn.com

Cover and Interior Design: JD Smith

CURL UP
PRESS

www.CurlUpPress.com

Dedicated to the Shadow creatives.

Let your dark horse run.

Contents

Part 3: Turn Your Inner Darkness into Words 179

Introduction.
What is the Shadow?

"How can I be substantial if I do not cast a shadow? I must have a dark side also if I am to be whole."

—C.G. Jung, *Modern Man in Search of a Soul*

We all have a Shadow side and it is the work of a lifetime to recognise what lies within and spin that base material into gold.

Think of it as a seedling in a little pot that you're given when you're young. It's a bit misshapen and weird, not something you would display in your living room, so you place it in a dark corner of the basement.

You don't look at it for years. You almost forget about it.

Then one day you notice tendrils of something wild poking up through the floorboards. They're ugly and don't fit with your Scandi-minimalist interior design. You chop the tendrils away and pour weedkiller on what's left, trying to hide the fact that they were ever there.

But the creeping stems keep coming.

At some point, you know you have to go down there and face the wild thing your seedling has become.

When you eventually pluck up enough courage to go down into the basement, you discover that the plant has wound its roots deep into the foundations of your home. Its vines weave in and out of the cracks in the walls, and it has beautiful flowers and strange fruit.

It holds your world together.

Perhaps you don't need to destroy the wild tendrils. Perhaps you can let them wind up into the light and allow their rich beauty to weave through your home. It will change the look you have so carefully cultivated, but maybe that's just what the place needs.

The Shadow in psychology

Carl Gustav Jung was a Swiss psychologist and the founder of analytical psychology. He described the Shadow as an unconscious aspect of the human personality, those parts of us that don't match up to what is expected of us by family and society, or to our own ideals.

The Shadow is not necessarily evil or illegal or immoral, although of course it can be. It's also not necessarily caused by trauma, abuse, or any other severely damaging event, although again, it can be.

It depends on the individual.

What is in your Shadow is based on your life and your experiences, as well as your culture and society, so it will be different for everyone.

Psychologist Connie Zweig, in *The Inner Work of Age*, explains, "The Shadow is that part of us that lies beneath or behind the light of awareness. It contains our rejected, unacceptable traits and feelings. It contains our hidden gifts and talents that have remained unexpressed or unlived. As Jung put it, the essence of the Shadow is pure gold."

To further illustrate the concept, Robert Bly, in *A Little Book on the Human Shadow*, uses the following metaphor:

"When we are young, we carry behind us an invisible bag, into which we stuff any feelings, thoughts, or behaviours that bring disapproval or loss of love—anger, tears, neediness, laziness. By the time we go to school, our bags are already a mile long.

In high school, our peer groups pressure us to stuff the bags with even more—individuality, sexuality, spontaneity, different opinions. We spend our life until we're twenty deciding which parts of ourselves to put into the bag and we spend the rest of our lives trying to get them out again."

As authors, we can use what's in the 'bag' to enrich our writing — but only if we can access it. My intention with this book is to help you venture into your Shadow and bring some of what's hidden into the light and into your words.

I'll reveal aspects of my Shadow in these pages but ultimately, this book is about you. Your Shadow is unique. There may be elements we share, but much will be different.

Each chapter has questions for you to consider that may help you explore at least the edges of your Shadow, but it's not easy. As Jung said, "One does not become enlightened by imagining figures of light, but by making the darkness conscious. The latter procedure, however, is disagreeable and therefore not popular."

But take heart, Creative. You don't need courage when things are easy. You need it when you know what you face will be difficult, but you do it anyway.

We are authors. We know how to do hard things.

We turn ideas into books. We manifest thoughts into ink on paper.

We change lives with our writing. First, our own, then other people's. It's worth the effort to delve into Shadow, so I hope you will join me on the journey.

Who am I and why did I write this book?

I'm Jo Frances Penn. I'm an award-nominated, *New York Times* and *USA Today* bestselling author of thrillers, dark fantasy, crime, and travel memoir as J.F. Penn. I also write non-fiction self-help for authors as Joanna Penn.

At the time of writing, I'm in my late forties and I live with my husband Jonathan and my two British shorthair cats, Cashew and Noisette, in Bath, England. I've been a full-time author entrepreneur since 2011 and before that, I used to implement accounts payable systems into companies across Europe, Australia, and New Zealand.

I first learned of Carl Jung's principle of the Shadow when I studied Psychology at A level, aged sixteen to eighteen, here in the UK. I later studied Psychology of Religion as part of my Masters in Theology at the University of Oxford (1994–1997) where I read Jung and many other perspectives.

In 2005, I did a Graduate Diploma in Psychology at the University of Auckland, New Zealand, and considered becoming a clinical psychologist. That's also the year I started writing my first book, which led to me becoming an author instead.

Over the years, I've continued to study elements of psychology and have woven its principles into my stories as well as my self-help books.

But of course, self-development is the journey of a lifetime and we are all a work in progress. I cannot claim to have solved all my issues, let alone brought everything that remains in my Shadow into the light.

I've been writing this book on and off for many years, first in my journals and then in various manuscript forms, but I backed away from finishing it until now.

Writing my memoir, *Pilgrimage*, unblocked a great deal and helped me overcome my fear of sharing more openly. I've also crossed a threshold into middle age and it's been a journey of such change that I finally feel ready to share this book.

While my personal experience will be different to yours, I hope you find this book useful as you face your own challenges on the path ahead.

A note on language

There has been much injustice and inhuman treatment of others committed under a racial dichotomy of black and white, but the language of darkness and Shadow used in this book is not intended to be construed as anything to do with race. It's a metaphor for that which remains hidden in all of us.

I am a White woman, and if I stand holding hands with everyone who reads this book of whatever racial background, our backs to the sun, we will all cast a shadow.

Trigger warning

This book may trigger you.

I hope it does.

Try to step away from whatever politicised reaction you might have to the word. All it really means is a reaction, and it's only by exploring uncomfortable feelings that we can go deeper into our creative process.

You won't agree with everything in this book, and you will experience denial: "Oh, that's fascinating, but it doesn't apply to me / my family / my culture / my faith / my situation." Notice those feelings as they may lead to the place you need to dig deeper.

Let yourself be triggered.

Then go write about it.

Balance your exploration with self-care

Treat yourself gently as you go through the book, as you would a loved one who is experiencing challenging times.

Things may come up for you, memories might emerge, and feelings may arise that need attention. You might encounter intense emotions, or none at all. You might dream a lot or have sleepless nights.

You might feel the urge to journal your heart out or write

in a different way than you do normally. You might want to go for long walks, be still in nature, or express yourself through other forms of art. Do whatever helps.

You don't need to share your insights with anyone. Give yourself time to reflect on the ideas and return to them later. I've been thinking about the Shadow for nearly three decades, so I know there are many layers to this process.

If you need professional help, please seek it out

This is a writing advice book, based on my personal experience, rather than for use in therapy.

I am not a medical professional, nor a trained psychologist, counsellor, or therapist. If you're struggling, please seek professional help.

What's in the book?

Part 1 goes into the various ways you can tap into your Shadow. Since it lies in the unconscious, you cannot approach it directly. You need tools to help reveal it in different ways.

You will find ideas here — ranging from personality assessments and identifying Shadow personas to mining your own writing and exploring your true curiosity — as well as ways to protect yourself so you don't get lost in the dark.

Part 2 explores how the Shadow manifests in various aspects of our lives. I discuss the creative wound and how it may still be holding you back in your writing life, as well as aspects of traditional and self-publishing, then expand into work and money, family and relationships, religion and culture, the physical body and aging, death and dying.

Part 3 explores ways that you can find the gold in your Shadow, and turn your inner darkness into words through self-acceptance, letting go of self-censorship, deepening character and theme in your work, and opening the doors to new parts of yourself.

While the book is designed to be read in order, you can also skip directly to the sections that resonate the most.

There are **Resources and Questions** at the end of every chapter that will help you reflect along the way.

You can answer these questions in your own journal or use the **Companion Workbook** if you prefer to write in a more structured way.

You can find it at:

www.TheCreativePenn.com/shadowworkbook

Right, let's get into it.

* * *

Note: There are affiliate links within this book to products and services that I recommend and use personally. If you buy through my link, I receive a small percentage of the sale at no extra cost to you, and in some cases, you may receive a discount. I only recommend products and services that I believe are great for writers, so I hope you find them useful.

Let your dark horse run

Although much has changed over the last two thousand years, human nature remains the same. Around 370 BC, the Greek philosopher Plato composed *The Phaedrus*, which includes an allegory of a chariot that has helped me frame the Shadow. Perhaps it will help you, too.

* * *

Imagine a Roman chariot drawn by two horses — a white horse and a dark horse. I am the Charioteer, and I am in the race of my life.

The white horse represents my rational self, the one society sees. My good behaviour, my industry, my hard work, my productivity, my scrubbed-clean, well-mannered good girl self.

She helps others. She's a peacemaker. She doesn't like conflict. She says the right things, reads the right books. She needs to be liked.

My white horse trots delicately along paved roads, aware of the fences and boundaries, never needing to cross them, remaining within the lines drawn by others.

My dark horse is a wild animal, wreathed in smoke and ash and flame.

She gallops across wide open spaces, leaps obstacles, smashes through fences, and avoids the paved and cornered world.

She runs free and will destroy herself, rather than be caged.

If both horses run together in the same direction, I can fly along, whooping in delight at the speed and power. But if they become unbalanced, the chariot begins to wobble.

When my dark horse stumbles, my white horse drives us hard along the highway, never stopping for rest.

But if she dominates for too long, my dark horse rears up and runs out of control, driving us towards the cliff edge.

My white horse has often been stronger.

I've always worked hard, got good grades, behaved well, earned enough money to support myself, paid my taxes early.

But the more I let my white horse dominate, the more my dark one rears up unexpectedly and takes over until she exhausts herself with all the things that nice girls shouldn't do.

When I became a writer, these two horses drove me once more.

My white horse writes non-fiction, helps others, wants to be useful, and responsibly manages a professional business. I'm grateful to have her!

My dark horse writes stories that tap into untamed darkness.

I've tried to muzzle her, strap her down, regulate her chaos.

But she rears her head, shakes her mane, stamps her hooves, paws the dirt.

Let me run.

Questions:

- What are the key aspects of your white horse?
- What are the key aspects of your dark horse?
- What happens when one or the other becomes dominant?
- How could you let your dark horse run creatively?
- How does it make you feel to consider that prospect?

Resource:

- *The Phaedrus* — Plato

Let your dark
horse run.

JOANNA PENN

Why explore your Shadow side?

It's not an easy or comfortable process to delve into Shadow, so why do it?

You will learn more about yourself and other people

"This thing of darkness I acknowledge mine."

—William Shakespeare, *The Tempest*

Self-development is the journey of a lifetime, a never-ending search for what it means to be human, a curiosity that drives us to learn and grow and change, to become more.

But self-development doesn't have to be all positive thinking and upbeat affirmations. It can also include an exploration of your darker side, and what you find there may accelerate your growth far more than bullish optimism.

Aspects of the Shadow can drive our lives without us even realising, but if we take the time to delve deeper and understand our hidden motivations, we can liberate ourselves and move into a new place in life.

If you have negative patterns in your life, this process may help disrupt them. If you can recognise your Shadow, you can express it in healthier ways than in self-destructive behaviour.

The gifts of the Shadow may help you overcome creative blocks that have held you back for years, and greater self-awareness may help you with confidence and self-acceptance. The gold in your Shadow may even become the source of your most powerful creative work.

Understanding these darker aspects of personality can also give you more empathy for others and give you an insight into why people behave in certain ways.

You will help yourself and other people

Humans love story in every form. We crave it.

But we don't want perfect people in perfect worlds experiencing nothing but a joyful, easy life. If a story starts that way, then we know it won't end well.

Story is how we learn to deal with life, how we vicariously experience the world. We all face challenges, and story in all its forms helps us navigate them.

Even the sweetest sweet romance has conflict, a storm that the characters must weather to achieve their happy-ever-after. The most inspirational memoirs feature people who go through hell to find their transformation. The children's books that resonate deeply are about overcoming adversity. Even most non-fiction books are written to help a reader tackle the obstacles of life.

Readers want darkness, even if they don't consciously know it, and so much of what we look for in art is the Shadow side. If you don't examine it, then how can you portray the true depths of human experience?

Of course, I don't want to fight to the death in the zombie apocalypse. I don't want to face dragons or demons or catch serial killers or blow up the Vatican. But I read books to experience those things vicariously, and somehow what the characters learn along the way helps me in real life.

If I'm scared about losing my family, then writing that threat into story allows me to experience that emotion and practice saving them over and over again. It releases the tension that builds up when I dwell on how powerless I am to help them in reality.

It's cathartic to witness characters overcome difficulties, face fears, and carry on even when they're wounded and broken. If we write these darker things, we can help others who need the same comfort.

David W. Wright describes his experience of bullying and being a victim of crime in his book *Into The Darkness*, and he talks about how reading comics and books helped him survive: "They showed me that no matter how much of a freak or an outcast I felt like, I wasn't alone... Without comics, books, and their promise of escape, I'm not sure I could have gone on."

He explains, "Writing has helped me channel some of that fear, hate and helplessness I felt. It's helped me find a place to put some of the residual pain I'm still working through. And it's helped me see outside myself, which has helped me connect to others I might not otherwise have connected with."

<u>Writing is like telepathy. Two brains connecting over time and space, a way to touch another mind through words.</u> If you can write your own pain, you can help heal someone else's, and perhaps even change the course of their life.

You will improve your mental health

"Write whatever you need to survive."

—Charlie Jane Anders, *Never Say You Can't Survive*

I've been journaling on and off since I was fifteen and while many of my notebooks are filled with inspirational quotes, happy memories, and love, many other pages contain words of anger, misery, fear, and self-doubt.

I often don't recognise the person I was when I wrote those things, even though it's clearly my handwriting. Who knows who I might be today had I kept those words inside and let them fester and rot?

But, because I wrote my dark thoughts down, they dissolved into the paper, captured between the threads. They felt real in the moment and then they were gone.

Writing your Shadow can help you process grief or anger or pain or anything you need, for however long it takes.

The blank page can become a counsellor without you ever having to speak a word aloud. It can be your secret therapist, and your words need never be published, unless you choose to share them.

You will deepen your author voice

Your author voice is what makes your writing *your* writing.

In many ways, it's indefinable, but over a number of books, over a number of years, you will discover it and your readers will learn to recognise it and return for more.

You can also deepen your author voice with elements of Shadow.

For me, it was about letting go of self-censorship and fear of judgment and allowing myself to write what I truly wanted to without letting my inner critic shut me down.

The first book where I really found my voice was *Desecration*, my fifth novel. That book means so much because I let myself be me. I needed time to discover this Shadow side, and I only uncovered it through writing.

> "Your writing voice is the deepest possible reflection of who you are. The job of your voice is not to seduce or flatter or make well-shaped sentences. In your voice, your readers should be able to hear the contents of your mind, your heart, your soul."
>
> —*Meg Rosoff*

You will write more authentically and be able to double down on being human

Since 2016, I've been writing and podcasting about the impact of artificial intelligence (AI) on authors and the publishing industry. This impact has only become more significant as the years have passed.

To be clear, I'm a techno-optimist. I use various AI tools as part of my creative process, and most of the services and websites I use as part of publishing and book marketing are powered by AI. I'm certainly not against using them, but they are *tools* to help us achieve our human creative goals and should be used as such.

While it's (almost) possible to generate an entire book with a few clicks, what is the point in doing so?

If a book doesn't come from a human creative spark, a call to write what we're curious about, what keeps us awake at night, or what is on our hearts, it's just another cookie-cutter product — and there are far too many of those already.

Life is short. We must write the books that only we can. The books that matter to us.

My recommendation has always been to double down on being human, to tap into our unique experience of the world, and to express what we consider important through our creative body of work.

We will never beat the machines at productivity and perfection, and I have no doubt that at some point an AI will write a technically 'better' book than me.

But that's okay.

Our flaws make us human. Our Shadow side makes us human. And that's the part other humans connect with in our writing.

If we accept that we are flawed, and so is everyone else, then why are we so scared to show it? Why do we resist putting our whole selves into what we create?

After all, we appreciate the depth of humanity in the paintings of Vincent van Gogh, visiting *The Starry Night* and marvelling at his vision while accepting that his mental health issues and family trauma made him the artist he became.

We read confessional poetry by Anne Sexton or Sylvia Plath *because* they shared their pain and flaws through their words.

We listen to songs by Eminem because he expresses his rage about the Shadow sides of family and fame and how this world breaks us apart.

In fact, we criticise art that is shallow or fake, and we ridicule wooden or one-dimensional characters in books or movies or TV shows. We demand depth in the art we love, so let us make art in the same way. If we can be even more human in our books, our words will resonate and readers will seek them out because they crave authentic experience.

In this book, I want you to see my quirks and imperfections — and yes, my Shadow side. That which makes me, me. I want to double down on being human and I hope it will help you do the same.

Kevin Roose explains this idea in *Futureproof: 9 Rules for Humans in the Age of Automation*. He gives the example of fingerprints left on the surface of a handmade ceramic mug, and how that piece is worth much more than one mass-made in a factory.

Roose explains his own approach: "For me, leaving handprints means that I start every reporting assignment by figuring out how I can put my unique stamp on it, and not have it feel like a generic story that any other reporter (or any piece of AI software) could have written."

We must find ways to instil the essence of our individual human experience and perspective into our books. Delving into the Shadow can help you do that in a deeper way.

Questions:

- Why did you buy this book? Why are you drawn to exploring your Shadow side?

- How do you think this process might help you?

- How might it help others?

Resources:

- *Futureproof: 9 Rules for Humans in the Age of Automation* — Kevin Roose

- "How to Write Fiction: Meg Rosoff on Finding Your Voice," *The Guardian*, 18 October 2011 — www.theguardian.com/books/2011/oct/18/how-to-write-fiction-meg-rosoff

- *Into The Darkness: Hook Your Readers (Without Getting Lost in the Dark)* — David W. Wright

- *Never Say You Can't Survive: How to Get Through Hard Times By Making Up Stories* — Charlie Jane Anders

- *The Art of Memoir* — Mary Karr

"IT IS BY GOING DOWN INTO THE ABYSS *that we recover the treasures of life.*"

JOSEPH CAMPBELL

Part 1: Tapping into the Shadow

1.1 How can you tap into the Shadow if it is hidden?

"Everyone carries a shadow, and the less it is embodied in the individual's conscious life, the blacker and denser it is. At all counts, it forms an unconscious snag, thwarting our most well-meant intentions."

—C.G. Jung, *Psychology and Religion*

The Shadow contains the hidden and unconscious aspects of self. You can't just shine a light at it and expect to figure everything out straight away.

We have created protective mechanisms to keep ourselves safe, so you need to work out ways to bypass them. Try to catch a glimpse of your Shadow out of the corner of your eye and approach it gently, from the side, as you would the wild dark horse from Plato's Chariot.

In the chapters that follow, I'll guide you through some approaches that might help.

1.2 What triggers you?

"Unless we do conscious work on it,
the shadow is almost always projected; that is,
it is neatly laid on someone or something else,
so we do not have to take responsibility for it."

—Robert A. Johnson, *Owning Your Own Shadow*

We all react differently to different things.

One person might have a sudden intense response to a situation or a headline or a social media post, while others don't even notice it happening.

There might be an emotional surge: anger, frustration, shame, fear, sadness, or embarrassment.

There might be a physical response: flushing hot or cold, sweating, speeding heart, feelings of discomfort, nausea or diarrhoea, weakness in the limbs, tightness, curling or hunching the body.

You might find yourself fixated on whatever it is, ruminating and thinking about it over and over, out of proportion to the way others might see it.

Take notice of when these things happen and under what circumstances, then consider whether your reaction might be related to aspects of Shadow. Of course, "sometimes a cigar is just a cigar," as the psychologist Sigmund Freud is reported to have said. But you might catch a glimpse of the Shadow this way.

Don't start with the big, contentious societal issues that trigger so many. They are much bigger than we can handle here.

Start with the smaller things, those more particular to you, and that are in your control. These tiny triggers might help you gain an insight into your unconscious, and if you can work through some of these, you can scale up to the bigger issues later.

* * *

I've been creating in public since 2008, so I'm used to comments and emails from people who don't know me, as well as negative reviews of my books. But some things trigger me more than others, usually when my Shadow recognises a grain of truth.

Someone once emailed and said, "You're boring and you create tepid content."

I'm English and we usually apply the word tepid to a cup of tea that is weak and not hot enough. You wouldn't want to drink it.

This might not seem like a big deal but the words made me flush with shame and denial. I was immediately angry — clearly triggered. I felt a need to reply and justify myself because I work really hard to create content that (thankfully) a lot of people find useful.

Years later, by considering what I have learned about my Shadow side, I can understand why that triggered me so much.

Returning to the analogy of Plato's Chariot, my white horse controls my content as Joanna Penn. I've certainly held back some things I might have said because I want to be useful and I want people to like me. I fear judgment and criticism and I don't like conflict, so I shy away from writing things that might attract it.

If I'm honest, sometimes my content as Joanna Penn *is* tepid. Not too hot, not too cold. Acknowledging why I reacted so strongly brings my fear out of the Shadow, and I can consider whether I need to make a change, and how I might do so.

These days, enough people find my Joanna Penn content useful that I don't need to change it, and there are plenty of other voices out there to listen to. I am also expressing myself with less of a filter through my patron community on Patreon.com/thecreativepenn, sharing things I don't on the main public site.

That email and many others have also helped me realise that many people in my community don't even know I write books and stories as J.F. Penn — which are *not* tepid or boring! It underscores my need to integrate that darker side of myself, one of the reasons I'm writing this book.

What do you judge or criticise in others?

> "What I criticise in others may be true of me."
>
> —David Richo, *Shadow Dance*

What types of people or particular behaviours do you judge or criticise?

Again, pay attention to anything that arouses a strong

emotional reaction, particularly if others don't consider it a big deal.

For example — and it seems ridiculous to write this — sometimes I judge others for having fun. I see people relaxing and enjoying themselves and I think they're lazy and wasting time when they should be working and achieving something with the day.

Lazy is a trigger word for me. It's something I would hate to be called.

But in examining the deeper reasons behind this, I can see that I've been rewarded in my life for my work. So much so that my self-worth is intrinsically linked to it.

If I don't work, I am not worthy, but this deep-seated attitude leads me to work to exhaustion. Not a healthy way to live!

I'll cover this further in Chapter 2.5, The Shadow in work. For now, it's an example to help you pay attention to even the little things — that may have a bigger issue lurking beneath them.

Questions:

- What triggers you? Consider the small things rather than the larger societal issues.

- How do you know when you're triggered? How does it feel?

- Pick one small thing that triggers you and investigate it further. Why might you react in such a way? What might lie behind that reaction?

- What types of people or particular behaviours do you judge or criticise that others don't find so objectionable?

- Why might you feel that way?

Resources:

- *Shadow Dance: Liberating the Power & Creativity of Your Dark Side* — David Richo

- *Owning Your Own Shadow: Understanding the Dark Side of the Psyche* — Robert A. Johnson

1.3 Examine patterns of repeated behaviour

> "How we spend our days is, of course,
> how we spend our lives."
>
> —Annie Dillard, *The Writing Life*

I started an IT consulting job straight out of university and one of my first roles was based in Brussels, Belgium. This was in the late nineties when the expense accounts were large and we were expected to work hard and play hard.

I enjoyed the trappings of the consulting life. The high salary, the status of the companies I worked for, the benefits of all-expenses paid travel. My ego was certainly happy and I had a lot of fun — at least I think I did. Binge drinking was part of the culture and it soon became normal for me. I can't remember much of that time, which makes it even more of a waste.

I kept drinking to release the pressure and at one point, I was taking caffeine tablets to wake up in the morning and painkillers to dull the hangover, before going out again that night. I repeated this behaviour with seemingly no ability to stop, despite swearing over and over that I wouldn't do it again.

I didn't have the time — or more correctly, I didn't make the time — to reflect on why I kept repeating this cycle. Some part of me must have understood that I hated my job. But it paid well, and I didn't know what else to do, so the golden handcuffs grew tighter over the years.

Finally, after a few years of this cycle, I tried running away.

I resigned and left London to travel around Australia in 2000, then I moved to New Zealand, but I needed to take consulting contracts to earn money. My pattern kept repeating.

As Jon Kabat-Zinn says, "Wherever you go, there you are." In the end, you have to solve the problem within yourself.

My repeated destructive behaviour was my Shadow acting out. My dark horse was not happy and the more I tried to rein her in, the more she tried to drive me off a cliff. I needed to look at my life and figure out how to change, which for me involved getting out of the job I hated.

I was an IT consultant on and off between 1997 and 2011, when I finally resigned for the last time. It took me fourteen years to break the cycle. I hope it doesn't take you as long.

Questions:

- What patterns of destructive behaviour do you notice in other people's lives?

- Are there patterns of destructive behaviour that repeat in your life? What might they be trying to tell you?

- How could you break the cycle and make a change?

Resources:

- *The Writing Life* — Annie Dillard

- *Wherever You Go, There You Are: Mindfulness Meditation for Everyday Life* — Jon Kabat-Zinn

"THIS THING OF DARKNESS,
I acknowledge mine."

WILLIAM
SHAKESPEARE,
THE TEMPEST

1.4 Look at the opposite side of personality tests

There are many personality tests, and they're all lenses through which to view yourself. They measure different things at different times, and shouldn't be seen as a box to constrain yourself with, but more as a tool to gain insight into your personality.

Most of them will give both positive and negative aspects of a particular personality type. While many people prefer to focus on the positive, you may glimpse the Shadow in the opposite.

There are two tests I have found most useful.

Myers-Briggs Type Indicator

According to the Myers & Briggs Foundation, the Myers-Briggs Type Indicator assessment is about helping people "identify and gain some understanding around how they take in information and make decisions."

There are different preference pairs:

- Extraversion (E) and Introversion (I), based on opposite ways to direct and receive energy

- Sensing (S) or Intuition (N) for different ways to take in information

- Thinking (T) or Feeling (F), which are opposite ways to make decisions and come to conclusions

- Judging (J) or Perceiving (P), which are different ways to approach the outside world and remain open to new information

I am INFJ, which stands for Introversion, Intuition, Feeling, and Judging. It's a rare type in the general population but more common in the author community.

The INFJ type includes some positive aspects, like access to creativity, insight, inspiration, and the ability to make decisions intuitively, as well as the desire to help others achieve their potential.

So far, so good!

But the negative sides give more of an insight into the Shadow.

INFJs can be perfectionists and control freaks, becoming frustrated when things don't go in the direction they want.

They can be overly sensitive and respond strongly when attacked or criticised.

Their introversion can go too far, leading them to be overly private, easily overwhelmed, and conflict averse to the extreme.

I recognise all of those things in myself, and by acknowledging what might lie in my Shadow, I can consider whether to accept my weaknesses or actively address them.

You can find the test at www.themyersbriggs.com

CliftonStrengths

The Gallup CliftonStrengths assessment is about discovering what you naturally do best and focuses on developing your strengths rather than fixing your weaknesses. It provides thirty-four different ranked themes, with your top five strengths being the most important.

After the test, you receive an extensive report which includes the positive aspects of your strengths and the blind spots that might hamper you.

My top five strengths are Learner, Intellection, Strategic, Input, and Futuristic, all of which are what Gallup considers strategic thinking strengths.

Towards the bottom of my thirty-four are the relationship-building elements, so I'm weakest in "building strong relationships that hold a team together." As an independent author with a core personal value of freedom, this is not a surprise!

Many authors have Learner among their strengths, so here's more detail on that particular theme. According to the Gallup organisation:

"You are drawn to the process of gaining knowledge and skills. You long to build on what you already know… You are determined to satisfy your need for knowledge as well as your desire to make measurable progress… You absorb all sorts of information from books, publications, or other written materials. You display a voracious—that is, never satisfied—appetite for knowledge… For you, a great day is one during which you have added new insights to your mind's storehouse of ideas."

Hell yeah, that's me, and I'm happy with that!

But the blind spots contain aspects of Shadow.

The Gallup description of the Learner strength warns that we can pursue learning for learning's sake, leading us to push learning on others or lose sight of our own goals. As they suggest, Learners must "be careful not to let the process of knowledge acquisition get in the way of your results and productivity."

I caught a glimpse of my Shadow here because to be called 'stupid' or 'dumb' or an 'idiot' is a real trigger for me.

I want to know all the things all the time. I want to be respected for my knowledge, and in the process, I might come across as superior or judgmental of those who are not as educated.

But of course, I can never learn everything. Even if I became a world expert in one domain, I will always be 'stupid' in another.

This focus has also damaged my health. I prioritised learning over physical activity and fitness, preferring hours hunched over my books or the desk. That decision, made every day for decades, eventually resulted in chronic pain and a shoulder injury purely from postural issues. A physical Shadow made manifest from the dark side of my primary strength, which I cover more in Chapter 2.8.

You can take the test at www.gallup.com/cliftonstrengths

If you want to learn more about Strengths, particularly as they relate to the author career, check out Becca Syme's books, courses, and coaching at BetterFasterAcademy. com.

I particularly recommend Becca's book *Dear Writer, Are*

You Intuitive? as that helped me discover aspects of my creative process that had remained hidden before.

Enneagram

The Enneagram is another kind of personality test which defines types by a core motivation — for example, The Achiever or The Peacemaker.

Though I haven't delved into this system myself, many writers find it useful. Comedy author Claire Taylor teaches how to use the Enneagram in fiction in her book *Reclaim Your Author Career*, as well as offering masterclasses and coaching in this area.

Questions:

- What are the positive aspects of your personality? What are your strengths?

- What are the opposites of these positive traits? How might they go too far? Do you recognise elements of those opposites in yourself?

- How can you prevent the negative attributes from taking control?

Resources:

- Myers & Briggs Foundation — www.themyersbriggs.com

- CliftonStrengths assessment — www.gallup.com/cliftonstrengths

- Strengths coaching and resources for authors — BetterFasterAcademy.com

- *Dear Writer, Are You Intuitive?* — Becca Syme and Susan Bischoff

- *Reclaim Your Author Career: Using the Enneagram to Build Your Strategy, Unlock Deeper Purpose, and Celebrate Your Career* — Claire Taylor

1.5 Be curious

"Let your curiosity be greater than your fear."

—*Pema Chödrön*

Curiosity is your "desire to know," according to the *Merriam-Webster* definition, and that "interest leads to inquiry."

It's a hunger to learn, discover, and explore. It's the feeling of wonder and intrigue that compels us to investigate further when we encounter something new, unknown, or unexpected.

You know when you're curious about something because your focus fixes on whatever you're interested in. You want to know more, and your mind tunes out other things while you satisfy your curiosity, however long it takes.

Curiosity is also driven by intrinsic motivation. You don't need to be paid or bribed into being interested. There's just something about whatever it is that draws you in.

As a writer, whatever kindles your curiosity may also spark a lot of ideas for your next creative project.

What if you don't know what you're curious about?

Back in 2006, I was working in Brisbane, Australia, as an IT consultant. After almost a decade in my professional career, I was desperately miserable.

I escaped into thriller novels on my train journey to work every day, but I never even considered that I might write fiction. After all, I didn't have any imagination, and I didn't have any ideas that might be the seed of a story.

I was writing a self-help book (which later became *Career Change*). It was based on how I deconstructed processes as part of my day job, so it didn't seem too far from what I could already do.

But writing fiction? That was never going to happen.

I literally could not imagine it back then, because I had lost touch with my curiosity and that was where my ideas were hiding. I had to turn off the social conditioning that had shrouded it for decades and actively work to tap into what I was interested in.

The mainstream education system mostly rewards children for obedience and passing exams based on rigid answers, rather than for curiosity and creativity. Curiosity can be disruptive in a classroom, so it's discouraged.

Sometimes we're shamed for asking dumb questions, or ridiculed for not knowing something, so we stop asking because we fear looking stupid or being embarrassed.

We're trained to value careers and pursuits that have more obvious outcomes, because clearly curiosity won't pay the bills. It's also potentially dangerous. We all know that 'curiosity killed the cat,' so we're discouraged from wandering off the well-worn paths that others tread.

We also don't have time in our busy lives. Curiosity more easily blooms when we leave unscheduled time for investigating different things, and in our over-scheduled lives, it can be too easy to stick to the routine. But as authors, we need to make the time.

Why you need to tap into curiosity

As an author, it's easy to get caught up in trends and try to produce what you think readers want rather than following your true inspiration. You may feel pressured to write about certain popular topics or in styles or genres that are (currently) commercially successful, to sublimate your curiosity into what others want you to focus on.

But when you suppress your authentic interests, your work may feel shallow, derivative, or lack a distinctive author voice. Given the expansion of AI tools, if you write generic work, it may also be unrecognisable from that generated by a Large Language Model.

Once again, I have no objection to the use of AI tools in the creative process, but the spark of curiosity must come from you.

The most impactful and enduring works come from authors who nurture their genuine curiosity and turn it into a body of work that stands out from the masses because it taps into a distinct set of interests that intersect in unique ways.

So how can we tap into our curiosity and maybe glimpse the Shadow there?

Schedule an Artist's Date

In her book *The Artist's Way*, Julia Cameron encourages the practice of a regular Artist's Date, a solo expedition where you explore something that might interest you.

Set aside time without expectations and try something new. Go to an art gallery or museum, take a creative class, or schedule an unusual experience, and just see how it goes.

Go alone, so no one else can tell you what to think or how to react. Watch for that spark of interest.

Back in 2006, this is how I broke out of my corporate limitations, the self-imposed boundaries I had put on my mind. I went on lots of Artist's Dates — excursions to a farmer's market by the sea, exhibitions at the modern art gallery, and a drawing class, amongst other things.

Slowly, I re-learned how to tap into the feeling of being curious and I rediscovered interests that were suppressed long ago because they were unacceptable in some way, or made others feel uncomfortable, or that I had discarded as useless for my corporate career path.

I started writing fiction in 2009 and published *Stone of Fire* in 2011, when we still lived in Brisbane, and it marked the beginning of a completely different career. I still go on regular Artist's Dates as part of refilling my creative well and my stories are often based on these experiences, which I include in my Author's Note at the back of my books.

Pay attention to how you feel in specific places

I travel a lot for book research these days, but I've always enjoyed discovering new places. Tapping into my curiosity around sense of place is also a key element of my creative process.

My fifth novel, *Desecration*, was a break-through book for me, and the first time I consciously let my dark horse run.

The spark of the idea came from visiting the Hunterian Museum at the Royal College of Surgeons in London. It's an anatomy museum with body parts in jars and gruesome medical equipment used by early surgeons in the time before anaesthetic.

As I walked around the exhibition, I had a visceral response to a wooden dissection board covered with plasticised human veins. My stomach turned in a combination of disgust and revulsion — but I also couldn't look away.

My mind teemed with questions about the person who had lain on this board generations ago: How did they die? Were they still alive as the surgeon cut into them? Who did the other body parts in jars belong to? How did modern science benefit from such brutality — and what is still brutal about medical practice today?

My curiosity about the dark history of anatomy felt taboo for a 'nice girl' like me, especially as I was not following a medical career. But I wanted to learn more.

I visited the Von Hagens Body Worlds exhibition filled with plastinated, exploded corpses in various poses, as well as the Mütter Museum in Philadelphia. I collected books on anatomy and corpse art, and read the Morbid Anatomy blog, as well as delving into how some people use body modification to express themselves. I investigated teratology, the study of developmental abnormalities, and researched Mengele's Nazi experiments.

I let my dark horse run in writing *Desecration*. It's not for everyone, but for those who are curious about such things, it's far more than a murder mystery novel.

What do you like to watch, read, or listen to?

We live in a golden era of content with unlimited options for consumption. Whether you prefer film or TV, gaming, music, books, or social media feeds, there is something for everyone.

When I was growing up in the 1980s and 1990s, we were limited in what we could consume. There were gatekeepers, arbiters of taste, who controlled what was produced and released. Some argue those were better times, but it's clear that those gatekeepers only represented a tiny segment of humanity and what people wanted.

Now there is unlimited choice and many niches where we can tap into curiosity. We may glimpse the Shadow in what we choose to consume — particularly when we're alone, when others cannot judge us.

We may also glimpse a Collective Shadow in what becomes a mainstream hit, or what resonates with us as a family, a couple, or among friends.

I rarely watch TV shows more than once, so when I do watch them again, it indicates there's something that resonates more deeply.

One show I've watched several times is *The Split*, a British TV series written by Abi Morgan, featuring divorce lawyer Hannah Stern, along with her two sisters and her mother.

The show tackles every angle of divorce and the complications of family relationships, love between sisters, and between daughters and mothers, as well as single parenthood. The characters are flawed and broken and yet, it's a joyful, poignant series that has left me in tears more than once.

In terms of how it might reflect elements of Shadow, my parents divorced when I and my brother were little. My dad later remarried and had three more children. I am the eldest — I have two sisters and two brothers — and my relationships with my siblings are precious to me.

Divorce brings pain, but it also brings a chance for a second life. I'm grateful for my parents' divorce because it gave me my siblings, as well as two nieces at the time of writing. I can't imagine my life without them, although, of course, there will always be the wonderful complications of family relationships to navigate.

I'm happily married for the second time, but my divorce from my first husband was difficult, as it is for anyone whose serious relationship ends.

Divorce for me is bittersweet. The wounds from my own experience as a child, and as an adult, are the foundation of my present happiness with Jonathan, and my blended family. So, perhaps it's not surprising that many of my novels feature sacrifice for family as a theme, as well as elements of second chance romance — nor is it surprising I enjoy *The Split*.

Buy paper books for the glimmer of an idea

In these days of digital consumption, it's easy to forget the serendipity of a physical bookstore, but sometimes we can find the seed of an idea in someone else's curiosity. I find the most interesting stores are the more curated book collections associated with art galleries or museums or hyper-local stores in specific places of interest.

I collect paper books that pique my interest even if I don't know how they might fit into a project. It may be years until whatever it is emerges into a work in progress, but if I have the book, then I know it will be useful somehow.

Some of the books I used to research this one have been on my shelf for years, but sometimes a book can be an immediate spark for an idea, like one I found at the Ets Haim Library, which is housed in the Portuguese Synagogue in Amsterdam.

We walked through the synagogue and library and then, as is my habit, I visited the small bookstore. There was a tiny selection of English-language books, but one title immediately leaped out at me: *Jewish Pirates of the Caribbean: How a Generation of Swashbuckling Jews Carved Out an Empire in the New World in Their Quest for Treasure, Religious Freedom, and Revenge* by Edward Kritzler. What a title!

That book and the synagogue itself contained the seed for what became my thriller *Tree of Life*, a race against time in the hunt for the Garden of Eden before a radical eco-terrorist group unleashes extinction on the entire planet.

Lean into your curiosity, trust your intuition, and you never know what could emerge.

Notice the Shadow in other people's art

If you're struggling to find elements of your Shadow, try noticing aspects in other creative works.

In Shakespeare's *Romeo and Juliet*, the young lovers have to hide their relationship, keeping it a forbidden secret. You can always catch a glimpse of Shadow in what is kept secret from others.

Their warring families are engaged in a blood feud that divides Verona, and each family demonises the other. There is no way this romance will ever be allowed.

The star-crossed lovers become enmeshed in even more problems with the deaths of Romeo's friend Mercutio and Juliet's cousin Tybalt, eventually driving the lovers to desperate action. As Romeo and Juliet try to keep their secret and escape their family feud, the story ends in tragedy and suicide. The Shadow side of love and family duty, indeed.

You can also include elements of other people's Shadow work in your own. In *Stone of Fire*, a key part of the plot was inspired by *The Red Book*, psychologist Carl Jung's journal, written during a breakdown and considered an exploration of his Shadow. It's an oversized red leather-bound book he filled with calligraphy of his thoughts and paintings of his inner life, visions, and dreams.

He wrote it between 1913 and 1929 and it was only published in 2009, which is when I bought an oversized full-colour edition, paying the most I had ever paid for a book.

The paintings inside include images of intricate mandalas, as well as mythological creatures. There's also a particular image of a grey stone with a pillar of fire rising from it, filling the room with billowing sparks and smoke as a man kneels in worship before it. Many of the ideas and symbols from *The Red Book* made it into *Stone of Fire*, including that very chamber.

If you're drawn to someone else's art — or if it triggers you or makes you uncomfortable — consider why and whether it might help you identify elements of the Shadow in yourself.

Questions:

- What sparks your curiosity?

- How do you know when you're curious about something? How can you lean into that even more?

- How could you make an Artist's Date a more regular part of your life to refill your creative well?

- How else can you fuel your curiosity?

- What do you like to watch, read, or listen to when you are alone?

- How might those things relate to your Shadow?

- In what ways can you glimpse the Shadow in other people's art?

Resources:

- *Desecration* — J.F. Penn

- Hunterian Museum at the Royal College of Surgeons, London — www.hunterianmuseum.org

- *Jewish Pirates of the Caribbean: How a Generation of Swashbuckling Jews Carved Out an Empire in the New World in Their Quest for Treasure, Religious Freedom, and Revenge* — Edward Kritzler

- Morbid Anatomy: Surveying the Interstices of Art and Medicine, Death and Culture — www.morbidanatomy.org

- *Romeo and Juliet* — William Shakespeare

- *The Artist's Way: A Spiritual Path to Higher Creativity* — Julia Cameron

- *The Red Book* — C.G. Jung. I have the beautiful oversized hardcover Liber Novus (Philemon) edition, translated by Sony Shamdasani, which you can find here: www.TheCreativePenn.com/redbook

- *Tree of Life* — J.F. Penn

- *When Things Fall Apart: Heart Advice for Difficult Times* — Pema Chödrön

1.6 Mine your writing for aspects of Shadow

We are writers. Our words are powerful.

We turn thoughts into reality through our books.

We figure out what the hell is going on with the world through our stories.

We learn what we need to by writing about it and sharing with others.

We heal ourselves one sentence at a time.

It makes sense that we can glimpse our Shadow side in the words we write.

You might catch sight of it in a draft of a poem, or a snatch of emotional writing in an old journal. You might discern an element from a character that you suddenly recognise yourself in, or a theme or symbolic motif that reappears again and again in your work.

You may find it in the writing you do in a deep flow state — the kind you read later and wonder who wrote those words.

Here are some ways to investigate further.

Read your existing writing with new eyes

You need some distance from your work in order to do this, and you need to feel emotionally separate from a book to read it with new eyes, but it's possible to see elements of Shadow there.

Examine your books of the heart, books written because you were inspired to write them or felt intuitively they were what you needed to write. It may not be so true with a product written to market, although, of course, there are traces of the writer in any book.

In early 2022, I rewrote my first novel, *Stone of Fire*, and re-published it, as well as sharing my lessons learned on my podcast and in my book *How to Write a Novel*. It was a useful exercise for understanding the development of my craft, but it was also eye-opening in terms of glimpsing my Shadow.

The story includes these elements:

- Sacrificing everything for family

- Love between sisters

- Travel to religious and historical locations, with musings on what religion and faith really mean

- Questions about good versus evil, and what happens after death

- A glimmer of second-chance romance

As I went through the rewriting process, it was fascinating to see how much of the story reflected things I didn't realise were so personal over a decade earlier when I wrote the first draft. My other books contain different aspects of Shadow that show the passage of time and my changing situation and thoughts.

Insights into your own work may not be obvious when you are still close to the book. Try reading your older work, perhaps even earlier drafts, and see what you can find.

Use journaling, free-writing, poetry, or other forms of instinctive, more emotional writing

Try writing specifically to access your Shadow.

Journaling involves scheduling time and writing your thoughts as they come up. It doesn't have to be in complete sentences, or paragraphs, or anything structured, although it can be. You can write based on prompts, you can use the questions in this book, or you can just write whatever comes into your head when you sit down for a journaling session.

You can free-write, which is a timed writing session where you keep your hand moving on the page. Don't stop writing, even if it's garbage or repetition, until the timer stops. That little bit of extra force means you might tap into a deeper side.

Poetry can be far more symbolic and metaphorical, so you may tap into something deeper if you write it — and of course, this is all first draft writing, so you don't need to show it to anyone. Try a poetry class to get started. I've done several over the years and have always found them useful.

As you go through this book, use ideas and phrases that trigger you to write on and see what comes up.

"If I don't write to empty my mind, I go mad."

—*Lord Byron*

Use AI tools to analyse your writing

If you're triggered by the idea of using artificial intelligence (AI) tools, that might reveal something in your Shadow around technology. Use free-writing or journaling to delve into that further and try to glimpse why you react so strongly.

If you're happy to try AI tools, I like the Claude 100K model at the time of writing, which you can access through Poe. com.

Given how fast the tools change, there will be other models able to analyse your writing, so research what might work for you.

Importantly, read the terms of service for a tool and decide whether you are happy before continuing to upload your work.

Personally, I'm not worried about working with these tools, but you must make your own decision (and I won't be doing tech support!).

I used the following prompt to analyse my thriller *Crypt of Bone*.

> "Can you please act as a story analyst with a specialty in Jungian psychology around the Shadow. What elements of the Shadow are in the attached book, *Crypt of Bone*?"

I uploaded the PDF print file of the book (around 65,000 words) for the model to analyse.

Here are a few of the notes it returned:

- The themes of fanaticism and people doing terrible things in the name of religion/God may connect to personal experiences with rigid belief systems or guilt over past actions.

- Morgan Sierra's self-destructive tendencies and attraction to danger could signify an unconscious wish for punishment or penance. Her struggles to trust others may stem from betrayal or abandonment wounds.

- The secret organisation Thanatos appears to be tapping into ancient, primal impulses related to violence, destruction and the fulfilment of prophecy. This aligns with ideas of the Shadow containing repressed drives that go against civilised norms.

- References to occult knowledge, curses and demonic forces hint at engaging with darker, more taboo aspects of human nature and spirituality that exist in the Shadow.

There were many more insights I found fascinating, and while I was aware of some of these things during the writing process, it's interesting to read an analysis of my work from an external source that imposes no judgment.

I then asked,

> "If you were a Jungian analyst with story expertise, what questions would you ask this author to try to understand their Shadow side? Please list at least fifteen questions."

Here are a few of them:

- Which characters do you most identify with and why? Which do you feel most different from?

- Do you see any of your own unaccepted qualities reflected in the villains? If so, in what ways?

- What inner forces or situations in your life have you felt a lack of control over?

- What inspired you to write about occult and taboo topics like curses and prophecies?

- Have you ever felt especially worthless, inferior, or like a failure in any aspects of life?

AI tools can often help by prompting us with questions to consider further in free-writing or journaling. Just ask them to ask you about a particular subject.

I mainly use ChatGPT Pro and Claude2 models at the time of writing as collaborative brainstorming partners for my work and in other aspects of my life.

If you want more ideas around AI for writing, then join the Facebook group
www.facebook.com/groups/aiwritingforauthors

Questions:

- How can you mine your writing for elements of Shadow? Which of these methods resonate?

- If you experience resistance towards any method, why might that be?

Resources:

- Writing Tips: Lessons Learned From Rewriting My First Novel Over a Decade Later with Joanna Penn — www.TheCreativePenn.com/rewritefirstnovel

- You can access Claude2 100K model through Poe.com as a paid subscription. You can also use ChatGPT Pro using the Advanced Data Analysis setting. These models change all the time, so please do your own investigation into what's current and make sure you're happy with the Terms of Service before use.

- I have interviews and resources on futurist topics, AI, and specific tools for writers if you want to explore further: www.TheCreativePenn.com/future

- If you want more ideas around AI for writing, join the Facebook group www.facebook.com/groups/aiwritingforauthors

1.7 Make a list of your Shadow personas

> "It is by going down into the abyss that
> we recover the treasures of life. Where you
> stumble, there lies your treasure."
>
> —*Joseph Campbell*

The things in your Shadow are there for a reason.

They protected us from harm at some point, and have a beneficial side, so it's not about trying to kill these aspects. Instead, the goal is to identify them, get to know them, and stop them from sabotaging us along the path ahead.

If you can catch a glimpse of your Shadow, if you can name an aspect of what you see, you can more easily find ways to deal with the impact in your life.

The Inner Critic

This is one of the most common Shadow personas for authors. It tells you that your writing is bad, that all of your ideas are unoriginal, and that no one will ever want to read your book.

The Inner Critic is useful in many ways, encouraging us to make our books the best they can be through editing and developing our writing craft, and keeping us humble in the face of success.

But it can go too far. It may stop us from creating altogether, or paralyse us with perfectionism, self-doubt, or fear, or prevent us from enjoying success.

If you can recognise the Inner Critic in yourself, that might help you identify a few more of your Shadow personas, the parts that help in some ways, hinder in others. If we can recognise them, we can modulate their influence.

I certainly have the Inner Critic, and here are more of mine to give you further examples.

The Workaholic

She works all the time and defines herself by her work. She doesn't play and struggles to relax unless she's exhausted or sick. She is driven to always be producing.

The Control Freak

She thinks and plans years into the future and tries to shape everything so it is within her control. She likes to do everything herself and struggles to let go of anything. She tries to control others, and that has damaged relationships before.

The Body Hater

She feels fat and ugly and chastises herself for ending up this way, then eats something to feel better. She struggles to walk down the street without comparing herself (unfavourably) with every woman she passes.

The Needy One

She really, really, really wants to be liked. She tries to avoid saying things that others might find offensive. She flushes with shame if someone says she is wrong or bad or anything that might mean she is not a nice girl.

These aspects of myself no longer lie in Shadow. I'm aware of them, but that doesn't mean they've gone away. They're part of me, and there are good and useful aspects of every Shadow persona. The point of the exercise is to understand why we act as we do, and try to stop these things from sabotaging us.

Questions:

- What are some of the personas in your Shadow? What defines their attributes? If you can't think of any, start with the Inner Critic, which is so common for writers.

- How do they sabotage you or harm you?

- How do aspects of each help you?

- How might they have developed?

Resource:

- *A Joseph Campbell Companion: Reflections on the Art of Living* — Joseph Campbell

1.8 Other ways to access Shadow

There are many other ways you can experiment with to try and catch a glimpse of your Shadow. I find writing works for me, so that's what I focus on in this book, but there are more ideas below that may help.

Some may trigger you, so consider why you react strongly to any of the ideas.

Go through Shadow Work or other forms of analysis with a therapist

There are many forms of therapy, and some therapists specialise in Jungian analytical psychology and can incorporate aspects of the Shadow in sessions. Exploring these difficult topics with an empathetic person can be the most supportive way forward, if you're able to talk about it aloud.

A therapist can provide a safe space to discuss issues without judgment. They're trained to address underlying causes, and can also unearth triggers and challenge denial or rationalisation in a compassionate way.

They can suggest other ways to help — for example, through dream analysis or reflective journaling — and also monitor development over time. They'll also know if you need additional support and make referrals if trauma or specific disorders require extra care.

Search for local therapists and practitioners and even if you don't find someone specifically for 'Shadow work,' you will find people who can help in different ways.

Meditation, breath work, body work

"In order to change, people need to become aware of their sensations and the way that their bodies interact with the world around them. Physical self-awareness is the first step in releasing the tyranny of the past."

—Bessel A. van der Kolk, *The Body Keeps the Score*

Writers tend to favour thinking and practices involving the mind, but there are ways to access the Shadow through more physical methods.

Even if you're not a regular practitioner of meditation, just sitting quietly without distractions can allow thoughts and images to bubble up freely from the unconscious. You might also notice sensations or emotions related to the material in this book.

There are specific breathing patterns you can do to induce states conducive to insight, and you can do these in meditation or yoga classes, or on your own. There are plenty of mobile apps to help if you prefer. I used the Headspace app while writing this book.

Different forms of bodywork can also help access elements of Shadow. Massage, energy field work, tapping, and techniques like EMDR can uncover issues in the unconscious.

Lean into your curiosity and try different things. You might be surprised by what you discover.

Psychedelic drugs and experiences with other forms of consciousness

I generally choose to alter my state of consciousness with coffee in the morning, and sometimes a gin and tonic or a few glasses of wine in the evening. But I'm fascinated by hallucinogenic drugs and how humans have always used them in sacred ceremonies to access different parts of consciousness.

There are many studies currently underway that demonstrate the positive and transformational use of psychedelics as part of therapy for trauma, PTSD, depression, and more.

The legality of such things differs by country and jurisdiction, so be sure to check if you want to investigate further.

You can read more detail in *How to Change Your Mind: What the New Science of Psychedelics Teaches Us About Consciousness, Dying, Addiction, Depression, and Transcendence* by Michael Pollan. It's also available as a documentary series on Netflix.

Tarot card reading

"Turn a card over and it can transport you
to the past, illuminate the present, or ask questions
of the future. It can help you listen to the whispers of
your subconscious mind, or hold up a lens through which
to look again, closer this time, at the experiences that
have made you who you are. Every card in the tarot is a
wildcard, a portal to the unexpected."

—Jen Cownie and Fiona Lensvelt,
Wild Card: Let the Tarot Tell Your Story

The mysterious imagery and symbolic nature of tarot cards can provide insights into the Shadow by sparking thoughts and ideas from the unconscious.

Cards represent archetypes and universal symbols, so reflection on their possible meaning may offer you insights. Each card has both positive and negative elements, so they can be used as a tool for analysis, or a prompt for writing.

When I went traveling in my mid-twenties, I spent several months exploring the outback in Australia as a solo traveler. I had a pack of Rider–Waite tarot cards with me as well as a book about how to interpret them. I read the cards for myself along the way, using them to spark my journaling.

Two cards came up for me again and again: The Moon and The Fool.

The Moon is depicted in the sky with a dog and a wolf howling up at it. I felt like it represented a time of change, waxing and waning every day, as well as contemplation, and also a certain wildness — howling at the moon — that I certainly enjoyed during that time.

The Fool shows a young man with a pack over his shoulder, a joyful dog at his side as he sets off on a lone journey over the mountains. It represents hope for adventure, and recklessness in pursuit of a goal that remains out of sight.

Both cards resonated with me then and although I no longer read for myself, I still have that pack here in my office.

Tarot can also assist in your writing process. If you're interested in reading more, try *Story Arcana: Tarot for Writers* by Caroline Donahue. I've also interviewed Caroline on The Creative Penn Podcast if you'd like to listen to a conversation about it.

Practice *Existential Kink*

"Just let failure and humiliation (and all the 'bad stuff'—anxiety and scarcity and fat and wrinkles and pain and ultimately death itself) be the cherished beloveds that they already are to you."

—Carolyn Elliott, *Existential Kink*

Carolyn Elliott describes various ways of accessing Shadow in her book *Existential Kink: Unmask Your Shadow and Embrace Your Power*.

Her basic premise is that "we human beings have a major habit of taking unconscious pleasure in the 'bad stuff' in our lives." Her process helps people "to acknowledge and 'own' this kind of weird underlying *desire* for and *pleasure* in stuff that they ostensibly hate and feel very frustrated by."

There is much more to the book, of course, and it contains meditations and practices for different situations with an emphasis on physical sensation and sexuality. Several people recommended the book to me, and while it didn't resonate with my ideas around the Shadow, I wanted to include it as an approach that may interest you.

Questions:

- Do any of these practices attract you or make you curious? How could you explore them?

- Do any make you uncomfortable or trigger certain associations, feelings, memories, or words?

- How might those give you an insight into elements of Shadow?

Resources:

- Creativity, Symbolism, and Writing With the Tarot with Caroline Donahue — www.TheCreativePenn.com/donahue

- *Existential Kink: Unmask Your Shadow and Embrace Your Power* — Carolyn Elliott

- Headspace app — www.headspace.com

- *How to Change Your Mind: What the New Science of Psychedelics Teaches Us About Consciousness, Dying, Addiction, Depression, and Transcendence* — Michael Pollan

- *Romancing the Shadow: A Guide to Soul Work for a Vital, Authentic Life* — Connie Zweig

- *Story Arcana: Tarot for Writers* — Caroline Donahue

- *The Body Keeps the Score: Brain, Mind, and Body in the Healing of Trauma* — Bessel van der Kolk

- *Wild Card: Let the Tarot Tell Your Story* — Jen Cownie and Fiona Lensvelt

1.9 Don't get lost in the darkness: Protecting yourself and others

> "The dose makes the poison."
>
> —*Paracelsus*

Exploring the Shadow is not without responsibility — for yourself and for others. It's not about unleashing the darkness so it consumes you, those you love, and your readers.

Look after yourself

My goal with this book is to help you write from your heart without fear, to discover new facets deep within, and put your whole self on the page. It's meant to be liberating.

But of course, things might come up that are difficult and you will need time to process them, so be careful and look after yourself.

You might find a daily practice of journaling, meditation, or walking useful to give your mind time to process.

If you feel overwhelmed, back off and give yourself space and time.

You don't have to go through this entire book in one session, and you certainly can't uncover and integrate your Shadow in one go. It's the work of a lifetime.

Take breaks and dip in and out. Your brilliant mind will work on things in its own time.

Maybe you'll dream more vividly. Maybe you'll find yourself writing something completely different, or expressing yourself through another artistic medium altogether. Maybe you'll feel like going for a long walk (or a *really* long walk as I did in *Pilgrimage!*). You can cry, be alone, whatever you need.

If you try something and it doesn't 'work,' then consider other options.

If you feel things are getting too dark, please seek out a professional. There are many counsellors, psychologists, therapists, and medical professionals who can help, at whatever stage of the journey you're on.

How do you know if you're getting lost in the darkness?

Some people think that by dwelling on terrible things, we might make the experience worse. That if we revisit our hurt over and over again, we cement it further in our minds and increase our pain. That maybe we even cause ourselves more harm than good by writing about it, or invite bad things into our lives by turning it into reality with our words.

I think that you will know by the way you feel — and that will shift over time.

There may be areas of your Shadow that are easier to work with at different times of your life. You may not know yourself well enough to write about them now, or you might not be ready to write about something that still hurts. But you can always start with the small things.

I'm an intuitive binge writer. I don't write every day. Sometimes I don't write for months.

The urge to write builds up and up and up until the idea is ready to emerge. I know when it's time to begin a book or finish one I've started, and if I haven't reached that point, I won't try.

Or I might try anyway and then swiftly realise that it's not the right time for that project. I might not know why.

Sometimes it's because I haven't fully processed whatever is behind it.

Sometimes it's because I'm not a good enough writer (yet) to put my chaotic thoughts into words.

This book is a good example.

I've been thinking about the Shadow since I first heard about it nearly thirty years ago, and I've considered writing a book about it for over a decade. But every time I approached it seriously as my next book to publish, I felt a push back, like when you hold two magnets near each other. The force is invisible, but it pushes them apart. I've written tens of thousands of words on the Shadow over the years and come close to finishing and publishing several times, but every time, I backed away.

Then my midlife travel memoir, *Pilgrimage*, unblocked a lot of issues for me and I felt ready to approach this Shadow book with new skills, having learned so much from the intimate experience of writing memoir.

There might be things you find in your Shadow that you feel an urge to write about now. Lean into that, for sure, but it might also take time. It might take decades, and that's okay.

Pay attention to the level of emotion you experience and back away as you need to. Is the process hurting or helping? Only you can decide.

As the Renaissance physician Paracelsus said, "The dose makes the poison." Something dangerous can be beneficial in small doses, but take too much, and you will lose yourself.

Protect others in your life

Delving into your Shadow is not an excuse to act in ways that may hurt others. In fact, doing this work will hopefully bring aspects of your behaviour into focus so you can change and avoid hurting other people.

It's also not about assigning blame to people in your past. It's about healing in the present and moving forward into the future.

In an interview on writing the Shadow, author Michael-brent Collings talked about incorporating difficult subjects into his fiction and how you have to be careful about your motives: "It matters what you're trying to accomplish. Are you trying to spread your pain to others? Well, that's not a good thing. Let's not do that. Are you trying to deal with your pain? That's a fine thing."

Write whatever you want in your private journals, but be responsible about publishing and consider the impact on others.

It may mean keeping silent until certain people are dead.

It may mean not publishing your work, or even mentioning that you have written something.

It may mean sharing your words with family members or others before publication to assess the impact and get permission.

Everything we write has consequences.

My personal rule is: Heal yourself. Don't wreck other people. There's a fine line and only you can walk it in terms of what you choose to publish.

> *Note*: I am not a lawyer and this book does not contain legal advice. If you have specific concerns about something you intend to publish that others may construe as defamation, invasion of privacy, or misappropriation of the right of publicity, please consult a legal professional.
>
> You can also find some details in the *Self-Publisher's Legal Handbook* by Helen Sedwick.

Protect your readers

If you publish your words, protect your readers by making it abundantly clear what they can expect.

You shouldn't need a trigger warning if it's apparent what's inside the book. You can do this with your book cover, your title, your genre or category in the bookstore, and your sales description. After publication, it will become even more clear in reader reviews.

If your book is dark and twisty, full of blood and violence, then give it a cover and a title that makes this clear.

If you write sweet, clean romance, then a chaste couple, a rounded font, and a clear category assignment helps.

The biggest problem comes if you mis-label a book and readers think they are getting one thing and then you shock them with something different. Yes, it's good to subvert genre tropes and surprise your readers, but not in a way that damages them.

Questions:

- How can you look after yourself as you delve into Shadow?

- How will you know if you're getting lost in the darkness? What are some of the signs?

- How can you protect others in your life?

- Where will you draw the line in terms of what you publish or share in public?

- How can you protect your readers?

Resources:

- How to Use Real People in Your Writing Without Getting Sued, Helen Sedwick — www.helensedwick.com/how-to-use-real-people-in-your-writing/

- *Pilgrimage: Lessons Learned from Solo Walking Three Ancient Ways* — J.F. Penn

- *Self-Publisher's Legal Handbook: Updated Guide to Protecting Your Rights and Wallet* — Helen Sedwick

- Writing From Your Shadow Side with Michaelbrent Collings — www.TheCreativePenn.com/michaelbrentshadow

Part 2: Aspects of the Shadow

2.1 You are not alone

> "Until you make the unconscious conscious,
> it will direct your life and you will call it fate."
>
> —*C. G. Jung*

While in Part 1, I suggested methods you could use to start to explore your Shadow side, here in Part 2, we'll examine how the Shadow can manifest in specific areas of life, which may help you investigate further. We'll consider the creative wound and how it may still be holding you back in your writing life, as well as aspects of traditional and self-publishing. Then we'll delve into aspects of work and money, family and relationships, religion and culture, the physical body and aging, death and dying.

Some of the chapters may trigger you or make you angry or upset. They will also help you prepare for difficult times — and hopefully, make you feel less alone when you find yourself in darkness.

The sections you respond to and/or want to skip may be the ones where you might find your Shadow hiding. Notice how you feel and try to work through the questions even if you don't think something relates to you.

The whole point of exploring your Shadow is to bring aspects of it into the light so you can process things, integrate them, grow, and move on. But don't worry, you don't have to do it all at once.

Let's get into the details.

2.2 The creative wound and the Shadow in writing

> "Whatever pain you can't get rid of,
> make it your creative offering."
>
> —Susan Cain, *Bittersweet*

The more we long for something, the more extreme our desire, the more likely it is to have a Shadow side. For those of us who love books, the author life may well be a long-held dream and thus, it is filled with Shadow.

Books have long been objects of desire, power, and authority. They hold a mythic status in our lives. We escaped into stories as children; we studied books at school and college; we read them now for escape and entertainment, education and inspiration. We collect beautiful books to put on our shelves. We go to them for solace and answers to the deepest questions of life.

Writers are similarly held in high esteem. They shape culture, win literary prizes, give important speeches, and are quoted in the mainstream media. Their books are on the shelves in libraries and bookstores. Writers are revered, held up as rare, talented creatures made separate from us by their brilliance and insight.

For bibliophile children, books were everything and to write one was a cherished dream. To become an author? Well, that would mean we might be someone special, someone worthy.

Perhaps when you were young, you thought the dream of being a writer was possible — then you told someone about it.

That's probably when you heard the first criticism of such a ridiculous idea, the first laughter, the first dismissal. So you abandoned the dream, pushed the idea of being a writer into the Shadow, and got on with your life.

Or if it wasn't then, it came later, when you actually put pen to paper and someone — a parent, teacher, partner, or friend, perhaps even a literary agent or publisher, someone whose opinion you valued — told you it was worthless.

Here are some things you might have heard:

- Writing is a hobby. Get a real job.

- You're not good enough. You don't have any writing talent.

- You don't have enough education. You don't know what you're doing.

- Your writing is derivative / unoriginal / boring / useless / doesn't make sense.

- The genre you write in is dead / worthless / unacceptable / morally wrong / frivolous / useless.

- Who do you think you are? No one would want to read what you write.

- You can't even use proper grammar, so how could you write a whole book?

- You're wasting your time. You'll never make it as a writer.

- You shouldn't write those things (or even think about those things). Why don't you write something nice?

- Insert other derogatory comment here!

Mark Pierce describes the effect of this experience in his book *The Creative Wound*, which "occurs when an event, or someone's actions or words, pierce you, causing a kind of rift in your soul. A comment—even offhand and unintentional—is enough to cause one."

He goes on to say that such words can inflict "damage to the core of who we are as creators. It is an attack on our artistic identity, resulting in us believing that whatever we make is somehow tainted or invalid, because shame has convinced us there is something intrinsically tainted or invalid about ourselves."

As adults, we might brush off such wounds, belittling them as unimportant in the grand scheme of things. We might even find ourselves saying the same words to other people. After all, it's easier to criticise than to create.

But if you picture your younger self, bright eyed as you lose yourself in your favourite book, perhaps you might catch a glimpse of what you longed for before your dreams were dashed on the rocks of other people's reality.

As Mark Pierce goes on to say, "A Creative Wound has the power to delay our pursuits—sometimes for years—and it can even derail our lives completely... Anything that makes us feel ashamed of ourselves or our work can render us incapable of the self-expression we yearn for."

This is certainly what happened to me, and it took decades to unwind.

Your creative wounds will differ to mine but perhaps my experience will help you explore your own. To be clear, your Shadow may not reside in elements of horror as mine do, but hopefully you can use my example to consider where your creative wounds might lie.

"You shouldn't write things like that."

It happened at secondary school around 1986 or 1987, so I would have been around eleven or twelve years old. English was one of my favourite subjects and the room we had our lessons in looked out onto a vibrant garden. I loved going to that class because it was all about books, and they were always my favourite things.

One day, we were asked to write a story. I can't remember the specifics of what the teacher asked us to write, but I fictionalised a recurring nightmare.

I stood in a dark room.

On one side, my mum and my brother, Rod, were tied up next to a cauldron of boiling oil, ready to be thrown in. On the other side, my dad and my little sister, Lucy, were threatened with decapitation by men with machetes.

I had to choose who would die.

I always woke up, my heart pounding, before I had to choose.

Looking back now, it clearly represented an internal conflict about having to pick sides between the two halves of my family. Not an unexpected issue from a child of divorce.

Perhaps these days, I might have been sent to the school

counsellor, but it was the eighties and I don't think we even had such a thing. Even so, the meaning of the story isn't the point. It was the reaction to it that left scars.

"You shouldn't write things like that," my teacher said, and I still remember her look of disappointment, even disgust.

Certainly judgment.

She said my writing was too dark. It wasn't a proper story. It wasn't appropriate for the class.

As if horrible things never happened in stories — or in life.

As if literature could not include dark tales.

As if the only acceptable writing was the kind she approved of. We were taught *The Prime of Miss Jean Brodie* that year, which says a lot about the type of writing considered appropriate.

Or perhaps the issue stemmed from the school motto, "So hateth she derknesse," from Chaucer's *The Legend of Good Women*: "For fear of night, so she hates the darkness."

I had won a scholarship to a private girls' school, and their mission was to turn us all into proper young ladies. Horror was never on the curriculum.

Perhaps if my teacher had encouraged me to write my darkness back then, my nightmares would have dissolved on the page.

Perhaps if we had studied Mary Shelley's *Frankenstein*, or H.P. Lovecraft stories, or Bram Stoker's *Dracula*, I could have embraced the darker side of literature earlier in my life.

My need to push darker thoughts into my Shadow was compounded by my (wonderful) mum's best intentions. We were brought up on the principles of *The Power of Positive Thinking* by Norman Vincent Peale and she tried to shield me and my brother from anything harmful or horrible. We weren't allowed to watch TV much, and even the British school drama *Grange Hill* was deemed inappropriate.

So much of what I've achieved is because my mum instilled in me a "can do" attitude that anything is possible. I'm so grateful to her for that. (I love you, Mum!)

But all that happy positivity, my desire to please her, to be a good girl, to make my teachers proud, and to be acceptable to society, meant that I pushed my darker thoughts into Shadow.

They were inappropriate. They were taboo. They must be repressed, kept secret, and I must be outwardly happy and positive at all times.

You cannot hold back the darkness

"The night is dark and full of terrors."

—George R.R. Martin, *A Storm of Swords*

It turned out that horror was on the curriculum, much of it in the form of educational films we watched during lessons.

In English Literature, we watched Romeo drink poison and Juliet stab herself in Zeffirelli's *Romeo and Juliet*.

In Religious Studies, we watched Jesus beaten, tortured, and crucified in *The Greatest Story Ever Told*, and learned of the variety of gruesome ways that Christian saints were martyred.

In Classical Civilisation, we watched gladiators slaughter each other in *Spartacus*.

In Sex Education at the peak of the AIDS crisis in the mid-'80s, we were told of the many ways we could get infected and die.

In History, we studied the Holocaust with images of skeletal bodies thrown into mass graves, medical experiments on humans, and grainy videos of marching soldiers giving the Nazi salute.

One of my first overseas school field trips was to the World War I battlefields of Flanders Fields in Belgium, where we studied the inhuman conditions of the trenches, walked through mass graves, and read war poetry by candlelight. As John McCrae wrote:

> We are the Dead. Short days ago
>
> We lived, felt dawn, saw sunset glow,
>
> Loved and were loved, and now we lie,
>
> In Flanders fields.

Did the teachers not realise how deeply a sensitive teenager might feel the darkness of that place? Or have I always been unusual in that places of blood echo deep inside me?

And the horrors kept coming.

We lived in Bristol, England back then and I learned at school how the city had been part of the slave trade, its wealth built on the backs of people stolen from their homes, sold, and worked to death in the colonies. I had been at school for a year in Malawi, Africa and imagined the Black people I knew drowning, being beaten, and dying on those ships.

In my teenage years, the news was filled with ethnic cleansing, mass rape, and massacres during the Balkan wars, and images of bodies hacked apart during the Rwandan genocide. Evil committed by humans against other humans was not a historical aberration.

I'm lucky and I certainly acknowledge my privilege. Nothing terrible or horrifying has happened to me — but bad things certainly happen to others.

I wasn't bullied or abused. I wasn't raped or beaten or tortured.

But you don't have to go through things to be afraid of them, and for your imagination to conjure the possibility of them.

My mum doesn't read my fiction now as it gives her nightmares (Sorry, Mum!). I know she worries that somehow she's responsible for my darkness, but I've had a safe and (mostly) happy life, for which I'm truly grateful.

But the world is not an entirely safe and happy place, and for a sensitive child with a vivid imagination, the world is dark and scary.

It can be brutal and violent, and bad things happen, even to good people.

No parent can shield their child from the reality of the world. They can only help them do their best to live in it, develop resilience, and find ways to deal with whatever comes.

Story has always been a way that humans have used to learn how to live and deal with difficult times. The best authors, the ones that readers adore and can't get enough of, write their darkness into story to channel their experience, and help others who fear the same.

In an interview on writing the Shadow on The Creative Penn Podcast, Michaelbrent Collings shared how he incorporated a personally devastating experience into his writing:

"My wife and I lost a child years back, and that became the root of one of my most terrifying books, *Apparition*. It's not terrifying because it's the greatest book of all time, but just the concept that there's this thing out there… like a demon, and it consumes the blood and fear of the children, and then it withdraws and consumes the madness of the parents… I wrote that in large measure as a way of working through what I was experiencing."

I've learned much from Michaelbrent. I've read many of his (excellent) books and he's been on my podcast multiple times talking about his depression and mental health issues, as well as difficulties in his author career. Writing darkness is not in Michaelbrent's Shadow and only he can say what lies there for him. But from his example, and from that of other authors, I too learned how to write my Shadow into my books.

Twenty three years after that English lesson, in November 2009, I did NaNoWriMo, National Novel Writing Month, and wrote five thousand words of what eventually became *Stone of Fire*, my first novel.

In the initial chapter, I burned a nun alive on the ghats of Varanasi on the banks of the Ganges River. I had watched the bodies burn by night on pyres from a boat bobbing in the current a few years before, and the image was still crystal clear in my mind. The only way to deal with how it made me feel about death was to write about it — and since then, I've never stopped writing.

Returning to the nightmare from my school days, I've never had to choose between the two halves of my family, but the threat of losing them remains a theme in my fiction. In my ARKANE thriller series, Morgan Sierra will do anything to save her sister and her niece. Their safety drives her to continue to fight against evil.

Our deepest fears emerge in our writing, and that's the safest place for them. I wish I'd been taught how to turn my nightmares into words back at school, but at least now I've learned to write my Shadow onto the page. I wish the same for you.

Questions:

- What did books and writing mean to you earlier in life?

- Do you recall comments or experiences that might have become your creative wound(s)?

- How might these hold you back as a writer now?

- How can you move past them?

- What are your nightmares? Have you written them into your stories?

- Can you trace the origin of why you write what you do?

Resources:

- *Bittersweet: How Sorrow and Longing Make Us Whole* — Susan Cain

- "In Flanders Fields," John McCrae. http://www.public-domain-poetry.com/ john-mccrae/in-flanders-fields-1461

- National Novel Writing Month — www.nanowrimo.org

- *The Creative Wound: Heal Your Broken Art* — Mark Pierce

- *The Successful Author Mindset: A Handbook for Surviving the Writer's Journey* — Joanna Penn

- Writing From Your Shadow Side with Michaelbrent Collings — www.TheCreativePenn.com/michaelbrentshadow

- Books I love — www.jfpenn.com/bookrecommendations

"UNTIL YOU MAKE
THE UNCONSCIOUS
CONSCIOUS,
*it will direct your life and
you will call it fate."*

C. G. JUNG

2.3 The Shadow in traditional publishing

If becoming an author is your dream, then publishing a book is deeply entwined with that. But as Mark Pierce says in *The Creative Wound*, <u>"We feel pain the most where</u> it <u>matters the most… Desire highlights whatever we consider</u> <u>to be truly significant."</u>

There is a lot of desire around publishing for those of us who love books!

It can give you:

- Validation that your writing is good enough

- Status and credibility

- Acceptance by an industry held in esteem

- The potential of financial reward and critical acclaim

- Support from a team of professionals who know how to make fantastic books

- A sense of belonging to an elite community

- Pride in achieving a long-held goal, resulting in a confidence boost and resulting self-esteem

Although not guaranteed, traditional publishing can give you all these things and more, but as with everything, there is a potential Shadow side.

Denying it risks the potential of being disillusioned, disappointed, and even damaged. But remember, forewarned is forearmed, as the saying goes. Preparation can help you avoid potential issues and help you feel less alone if you encounter them.

The myth of success… and the reality of experience

There is a pervasive myth of success in the traditional publishing industry, perpetuated by media reporting on brand name and breakout authors, those few outliers whose experience is almost impossible to replicate.

Because of such examples, many new traditionally published authors think that their first book will hit the top of the bestseller charts or win an award, as well as make them a million dollars — or at least a big chunk of cash. They will be able to leave their job, write in a beautiful house overlooking the ocean, and swan around the world attending conferences, while writing more bestselling books. It will be a charmed life.

But that is not the reality.

Perhaps it never was.

Even so, the life of a traditionally published author represents a mythic career with the truth hidden behind a veil of obscurity.

In April 2023, *The Bookseller* in the UK reported that "more than half of authors (54%) responding to a survey on their experiences of publishing their debut book have said the process negatively affected their mental health. Though views were mixed, just 22%… described a positive experience overall… Among the majority who said they had a negative experience of debut publication, anxiety, stress, depression and 'lowered' self-esteem were cited, with lack of support, guidance or clear and professional communication from their publisher among the factors that contributed."

Many authors who have negative experiences around publishing will push them into the Shadow with denial or self-blame, preferring to keep the dream alive. They won't talk about things in public as this may negatively affect their careers, but private discussions are often held in the corners of writing conferences or social media groups online.

Some of the issues are as follows:

Repeated rejection by agents and publishers may lead to the author thinking they are not good enough as a writer, which can lead to feeling unworthy as a person. If an author gets a deal, the amount of advance and the name and status of the publisher compared to others create a hierarchy that impacts self-esteem.

A deal for a book may be much lower than an author might have been expecting, with low or no advance, and the resulting experience with the publisher beneath expectations.

The **launch process** may be disappointing, and the book may appear without fanfare, with few sales and no best-seller chart position.

In *The Bookseller* report, one author described her launch day as

> "a total wasteland… You have expectations about what publication day will be like, but in reality, nothing really happens."

The book may receive negative reviews by critics or readers or more publicly on social media, which can make an author feel attacked.

The book might not sell as well as expected, and the author may feel like it's their fault. Commercial success can sometimes feel tied to self-worth and an author can't help but compare their sales to others, with resulting embarrassment or shame.

The **communication from the publisher** may be less than expected. One author in *The Bookseller* report said,

> "I was shocked by the lack of clarity and shared information and the cynicism that underlies the superficial charm of this industry."

There is often more of a focus on debut authors in publishing houses, so those who have been writing and publishing in the midlist for years can feel **ignored and undervalued**.

In *The Bookseller* report, 48 percent of authors reported "their publisher supported them for less than a year," with one saying,

> "I got no support and felt like a commodity, like the team had moved on completely to the next book."

If an author is not successful enough, **the next deal may be lower than the last**, less effort is made with marketing, and they may be let go.

In *The Bookseller* report, "six authors—debut and otherwise—cited being dropped by their publisher, some with no explanation."

Even if everything goes well and an author is considered successful by others, they may experience **imposter syndrome**, feeling like a fraud when speaking at conferences or doing book signings.

And the list goes on …

All these things can lead to feelings of shame, inadequacy, and embarrassment; loss of status in the eyes of peers; and a sense of failure if a publishing career is not successful enough.

The author feels like it's their fault, like they weren't good enough — although, of course, the reality is that the conditions were not right at the time. A failure of a book is not a failure of the person, but it can certainly feel like it!

When you acknowledge the Shadow, it loses its power

Despite all the potential negatives of traditional publishing, if you know what could happen, you can mitigate them. You can prepare yourself for various scenarios and protect yourself from potential fall-out.

It's clear from *The Bookseller* report that too many authors have unrealistic expectations of the industry.

But publishers are businesses, not charities.

It's not their job to make you feel good as an author. It's their job to sell books and pay you. The best thing they can do is to continue to be a viable business so they can keep putting books on the shelves and keep paying authors, staff, and company shareholders.

When you license your creative work to a publisher, you're giving up control of your intellectual property in exchange for money and status.

Bring your fears and issues out of the Shadow, acknowledge them, and deal with them early, so they do not get pushed down and re-emerge later in blame and bitterness.

Educate yourself on the business of publishing. Be clear on what you want to achieve with any deal. Empower yourself as an author, take responsibility for your career, and you will have a much better experience.

Questions:

- What dreams do you have — or did you have — around traditional publishing?

- What are the pros and cons of traditional publishing for you?

- Why do you value traditional publishing?

- What triggers you in this area? What do you get angry about, or deny exists, or criticise in other authors, or rant about in private?

- How do you feel when you compare your author career to others? How might those feelings reveal something about your Shadow?

- How can you make your publishing experience more empowering?

Resources:

- *The Successful Author Mindset: A Handbook for Surviving the Writer's Journey* — Joanna Penn

- "Survey finds debut authors struggle with lack of support," *The Bookseller*, 24 April 2023 — www.thebookseller.com/news/bookseller-survey-finds-debut-authors-struggle-with-lack-of-support

- Want a community of traditionally published authors? There are organisations in most countries. In the UK, check out The Society of Authors, and The Author's Guild in the USA.

2.4 The Shadow in self-publishing or being an indie author

Self-publishing, or being an independent (indie) author, can be a fantastic, pro-active choice for getting your book into the world. Holding your first book in your hand and saying "I made this" is pretty exciting, and even after more than forty books, I still get excited about seeing ideas in my head turn into a physical product in the world.

Self-publishing can give an author:

- Creative control over what to write, editorial and cover design choices, when and how often to publish, and how to market

- Empowerment over your author career and the ability to make choices that impact success without asking for permission

- Ownership and control of intellectual property assets, resulting in increased opportunity around licensing and new markets

- Independence and the potential for recurring income for the long term

- Autonomy and flexibility around timelines, publishing options, and the ability to easily pivot into new genres and business models

- Validation based on positive reader reviews and money earned

- Personal growth and learning through the acquisition of new skills, resulting in a boost in confidence and self-esteem

- A sense of belonging to an active and vibrant community of indie authors around the world

Being an indie author can give you all this and more, but once again, there is a Shadow side and preparation can help you navigate potential issues.

The myth of success… and the reality of experience

As with traditional publishing, the indie author world has perpetuated a myth of success in the example of the breakout indie author like E.L. James with *Fifty Shades of Grey*, Hugh Howey with *Wool*, or Andy Weir with *The Martian*.

The emphasis on financial success is also fuelled online by authors who share screenshots showing six-figure months or seven-figure years, without sharing marketing costs and other outgoings, or the amount of time spent on the business.

Yes, these can inspire some, but it can also make others feel inadequate and potentially lead to bad choices about how to publish and market based on comparison.

The indie author world is full of just as much ego and a desire for status and money as traditional publishing.

This is not a surprise!

Most authors, regardless of publishing choices, are a mix of massive ego and chronic self-doubt. We are human, so the same issues will re-occur. A different publishing method doesn't cure all ills.

Some of the issues are as follows:

You learn everything you need to know about writing and editing, only to find that you need to **learn a whole new set of skills** in order to self-publish and market your book. This can take a lot of time and effort you did not expect, and things change all the time so you have to keep learning.

Being in control of every aspect of the publishing process, from writing to cover design to marketing, can be overwhelming, leading to indecision, perfectionism, stress, and even burnout as you try to do all the things.

You try to find people to help, but **building your team is a challenge**, and working with others has its own difficulties.

People say negative things about self-publishing that may arouse feelings of **embarrassment or shame**. These might be little niggles, but they needle you, nonetheless. You wonder whether you made the right choice.

You struggle with self-doubt and if you go to an event with traditional published authors, you compare yourself to them and feel like an imposter.

Are you good enough to be an author if a traditional publisher hasn't chosen you?

Is it just vanity to self-publish?

Are your books unworthy?

Even though you worked with a professional editor, you still get one-star reviews and **you hate criticism from readers**. You wonder whether you're wasting your time.

You might be **ripped off** by an author services company who promise the world, only to leave you with a pile of printed books in your garage and no way to sell them.

When you finally publish your book, it languishes at the bottom of the charts while other authors hit the top of the list over and over, raking in the cash while you are **left out of pocket**.

You don't admit to over-spending on marketing as it makes you ashamed.

You resist book marketing and make critical comments about writers who embrace it. You believe that quality rises to the top and if a book is good enough, people will buy it anyway. This can **lead to disappointment and disillusionment when you launch** your book and it doesn't sell many copies because nobody knows about it.

You try to do what everyone advises, but **you still can't make decent money** as an author.

You're jealous of other authors' success and put it down to them 'selling out' or writing things you can't or 'using AI' or 'using a ghostwriter' or having a specific business model you consider impossible to replicate.

And the list goes on…

When you acknowledge the Shadow, it loses its power

Being in control of your books and your author career is a double-edged sword.

Traditionally published authors can criticise their publishers or agents or the marketing team or the bookstores or the media, but indie authors have to take responsibility for it all.

Sure, we can blame 'the algorithms' or social media platforms, or criticise other authors for having more experience or more money to invest in marketing, or attribute their success to writing in a more popular genre — but we also know there are always people who do well regardless of the challenges.

Once more, we're back to acknowledging and integrating the Shadow side of our choices. We are flawed humans. There will always be good times and bad, and difficulties to offset the high points. This too shall pass, as the old saying goes.

I know that being an indie author has plenty of Shadow. I've been doing this since 2008 and despite the hard times, I'm still here.

I'm still writing. I'm still publishing.

This life is not for everyone, but it's my choice. You must make yours.

Questions:

- What dreams do you have — or did you have — around self-publishing or being an indie author?

- What are the pros and cons of self-publishing for you?

- Why do you value self-publishing?

- What triggers you in this area? What do you get angry about, or deny exists, or criticise in other authors, or rant about in private?

- How do you feel when you compare your author career to others? How might those feelings reveal something about your Shadow?

- How can you make your experience more empowering?

Resources:

- *Successful Self-Publishing: How to Self-Publish and Market Your Book* — Joanna Penn

- *The Successful Author Mindset: A Handbook for Surviving the Writer's Journey* — Joanna Penn

- Want a community of indie authors? Check out the Alliance of Independent Authors — www.TheCreativePenn.com/alliance

2.5 The Shadow in work

You work hard. You make a living.

Nothing wrong with that attitude, right?

It's what we're taught from an early age and, like so much of life, it's not a problem until it goes to extremes.

Not achieving what you want to? Work harder. Can't get ahead? Work harder. Not making a good enough living? Work harder.

People who don't work hard are lazy. They don't deserve handouts or benefits. People who don't work hard aren't useful, so they are not valued members of our culture and community.

But what about the old or the sick, the mentally ill, or those with disabilities? What about children?

What about the unemployed? The under-employed?

What about those who are — or will be — displaced by technology, those called "the useless class" by historian Yuval Noah Harari in his book *Homo Deus*?

What if we become one of these in the future?

Who am I if I cannot work?

The Shadow side of my attitude to work became clear when I caught COVID in the summer of 2021.

I was the sickest I'd ever been. I spent two weeks in bed unable to even think properly, and six weeks after that, I was barely able to work more than an hour a day before lying in the dark and waiting for my energy to return. I was limited in what I could do for another six months after that. At times, I wondered if I would ever get better.

Jonathan kept urging me to be patient and rest.

But I don't know how to rest. I know how to work and how to sleep.

I can do 'active rest,' which usually involves walking a long way or traveling somewhere interesting, but those require a stronger mind and body than I had during those months.

It struck me that even if I recovered from the virus, I had glimpsed my future self.

One day, I *will* be weak in body and mind.

If I'm lucky, that will be many years away and hopefully for a short time before I die — but it will happen.

I am an animal. I will die. My body and mind will pass on and I will be no more.

Before then I will be weak.

Before then, I will be useless.

Before then, I will be a burden.

I will not be able to work… But who am I if I cannot work? What is the point of me?

I can't answer these questions right now, because although I recognise them as part of my Shadow, I've not progressed far enough to have dealt with them entirely.

My months of COVID gave me some much-needed

empathy for those who cannot work, even if they want to. We need to reframe what work is as a society, and value humans for different things, especially as technology changes what work even means. That starts with each of us.

> "Illness, affliction of body and soul, can be life-altering. It has the potential to reveal the most fundamental conflict of the human condition: the tension between our infinite, glorious dreams and desires and our limited, vulnerable, decaying physicality."

—Connie Zweig, *The Inner Work of Age: Shifting from Role to Soul*

Questions:

- What does 'work' mean to you?

- Where have those opinions come from?

- How will you define yourself if you cannot work?

- What aspects of work might be in your Shadow?

- What might be some healthier ways to look at work? Are there changes you can make in your life now to incorporate these?

Resources:

- *Homo Deus: A Brief History of Tomorrow* — Yuval Noah Harari

- *The Inner Work of Age: Shifting from Role to Soul* — Connie Zweig

2.6 The Shadow in money

In the Greek myth, King Midas was a wealthy ruler who loved gold above all else. His palace was adorned with golden sculptures and furniture, and he took immense pleasure in his riches. Yet, despite his vast wealth, he yearned for more.

After doing a favour for Dionysus, the god of wine and revelry, Midas was granted a single wish. Intoxicated by greed, he wished that everything he touched would turn to gold — and it was so.

At first, it was a lot of fun.

Midas turned everything else in his palace to gold, even the trees and stones of his estate. After a morning of turning things to gold, he fancied a spot of lunch.

But when he tried to eat, the food and drink turned to gold in his mouth. He became thirsty and hungry — and increasingly desperate.

As he sat in despair on his golden throne, his beloved young daughter ran to comfort him. For a moment, he forgot his wish — and as she wrapped her arms around him and kissed his cheek, she turned into a golden statue, frozen in precious metal.

King Midas cried out to the gods to forgive him, to reverse the wish.

He renounced his greed and gave away all his wealth, and his daughter was returned to life.

The moral of the story: Wealth and greed are bad.

In Charles Dickens's *A Christmas Carol*, Ebenezer Scrooge is described as a "squeezing, wrenching, grasping, scraping, clutching, covetous, old sinner." He's wealthy but does not share, considering Christmas spending to be frivolous and giving to charity to be worthless. He's saved by a confrontation with his lonely future and becomes a generous man and benefactor of the poor.

Wealth is good if you share it with others.

The gospel of Matthew, chapter 25: 14-30, tells the parable of the bags of gold, in which a rich man goes on a journey and entrusts his servants with varying amounts of gold. On his return, the servants who multiplied the gold through their efforts and investments are rewarded, while the one who merely returned the gold with no interest is punished:

> "For whoever has will be given more, and they will have an abundance. Whoever does not have, even what they have will be taken from them."

Making money is good, making more money is even better. If you can't make any money, you don't deserve to have any.

Within the same gospel, in Matthew 19:24, Jesus encounters a wealthy man and tells him to sell all his possessions and give the money to the poor, which the man is unable to do. Jesus says,

> "It is easier for a camel to go through the eye of a needle than for someone who is rich to enter the kingdom of God."

Wealth is bad. Give it all away and you'll go to heaven.

With all these contradictory messages, no wonder we're so conflicted about money!

How do you think and feel about money?

While money is mostly tied to our work, it's far more than just a transactional object for most people. It's loaded with complex symbolism and judgment handed down by family, religion, and culture.

You are likely to find elements of Shadow by examining your attitudes around money.

Consider which of the following statements resonate with you or write your own.

- Money stresses me out. I don't want to talk about it or think about it.

- Some people hoard money, so there is inequality. Rich people are bad and we should take away their wealth and give it to the poor.

- I can never make enough money to pay the bills, or to give my family what I want to provide.

- Money doesn't grow on trees.

- It's wasteful to spend money as you might need it later, so I'm frugal and don't spend money unless absolutely necessary.

- It is better and more ethical to be poor than to be rich.

- I want more money. I read books and watch TV shows about rich people because I want to live like that. Sometimes I spend too much on things for a glimpse of what that might be like.

- I buy lottery tickets and dream of winning all that money.

- I'm jealous of people who have money. I want more of it and I resent those who have it.

- I'm no good with money. I don't like to look at my bank statement or credit card statement. I live off my overdraft and I'm in debt. I will never earn enough to get out of debt and start saving, so I don't think too much about it.

- I don't know enough about money. Talking about it makes me feel stupid, so I just ignore it. People like me aren't educated about money.

- I need to make more money. If I can make lots of money, then people will look up to me. If I make lots of money, I will be secure, nothing can touch me, I will be safe.

- I never want to be poor. I would be ashamed to be poor. I will never go on benefits. My net worth is my self worth.

- Money is good. We have the best standard of living in history because of the increase in wealth over time. Even the richest kings of history didn't have what many middle-class people have today in terms of access to food, water, technology, healthcare, education, and more.

- The richest people give the most money to the poor through taxation and charity, as well as through building companies that employ people and invent new things. The very richest give away much of their fortunes. They provide far more benefit to the world than the poor.

- I love money. Money loves me. Money comes easily and quickly to me. I attract money in multiple streams of income. It flows to me in so many ways. I spend money. I invest money. I give money. I'm happy and grateful for all that I receive.

The Shadow around money for authors in particular

Many writers and other creatives have issues around money and wealth. How often have you heard the following, and which do you agree with?

- You can't make money with your writing. You'll be a poor author in a garret, a starving artist.

- You can't write 'good quality' books and make money.

- If you make money writing, you're a hack, you're selling out. You are less worthy than someone who writes only for the Muse. Your books are commercial, not artistic.

- If you spend money on marketing, then your books are clearly not good enough to sell on their own.

- My agent / publisher / accountant / partner deals with the money side. I like to focus on the creative side of things.

My money story

> *Note:* This is not financial or investment advice. Please talk to a professional about your situation.

I've had money issues over the years — haven't we all! But I have been through a (long) process to bring money out of my Shadow and into the light. There will always be more to discover, but hopefully my money story will help you, or at least give you an opportunity to reflect.

Like most people, I didn't grow up with a lot of money. My parents started out as teachers, but later my mum — who I lived with, along with my brother — became a change management consultant, moving to the USA and earning a lot more. I'm grateful that she moved into business because her example changed the way I saw money and provided some valuable lessons.

(1) You can change your circumstances by learning more and then applying that to leverage opportunity into a new job or career

Mum taught English at a school in Bristol when we moved back from Malawi, Africa, in the mid '80s but I remember how stressful it was for her, and how little money she made. She wanted a better future for us all, so she took a year out to do a master's degree in management.

In the same way, when I wanted to change careers and leave consulting to become an author, I spent time and money learning about the writing craft and the business of publishing. I still invest a considerable chunk on continuous learning, as this industry changes all the time.

(2) You might have to downsize in order to leap forward

The year my mum did her degree, we lived in the attic of another family's house; we ate a lot of one-pot casserole and our treat was having a Yorkie bar on the walk back from the museum.

We wore hand-me-down clothes, and I remember one day at school when another girl said I was wearing her dress. I denied it, of course, but there in back of the dress was her name tag. I still remember her name and I can still feel that flush of shame and embarrassment. I was determined to never feel like that again. But what I didn't realize at the time was that I was also learning the power of downsizing.

Mum got her degree and then a new job in management in Bristol. She bought a house, and we settled for a few years. I had lots of different jobs as a teenager. My favourite was working in the delicatessen because we got a free lunch made from delicious produce. After I finished A-levels, I went to the University of Oxford, and my mum and brother moved to the USA for further opportunities.

I've downsized multiple times over the years, taking a step back in order to take a step forward. The biggest was in 2010 when I decided to leave consulting. Jonathan and I sold our three-bedroom house and investments in Brisbane, Australia, and rented a one-bedroom flat in London, so we could be debt-free and live on less while I built up a new career. It was a decade before we bought another house.

(3) Comparison can be deadly: there will always be people with more money than you

Oxford was an education in many ways and relevant to this chapter is how much I didn't know about things people with money took for granted.

I learned about formal hall and wine pairings, and how to make a perfect gin and tonic. I ate smoked salmon for the first time. I learned how to fit in with people who had a *lot* more money than I did, and I definitely wanted to have money of my own to play with.

(4) Income is not wealth

You can earn lots but have nothing to show for it after years of working. I learned this in my first few years of IT consulting after university. I earned a great salary and then went contracting, earning even more money at a daily rate.

I had a wonderful time. I traveled, ate and drank and generally made merry, but I always had to go back to the day job when the money ran out. I couldn't work out how I could ever stop this cycle.

Then I read *Rich Dad, Poor Dad* by Robert Kiyosaki, a book I still recommend, especially if you're from a family that values academic over financial education. I learned how to escape the rat race by building and/or accumulating assets that pay even when you're not working. It was a revelation!

The 'poor dad' in the book is a university professor. He knows so much about so many things, but he ends up poor as he did not educate himself about money. The 'rich dad' has little formal education, but he knows about money and wealth because he learned about it, as we can do at any stage in our lives.

(5) Not all investments suit every person, so find the right one for you

Once I discovered the world of investing, I read all the books and did courses and in-person events. I joined communities and I up-skilled big time.

Of course, I made mistakes and learned lots along the way.

I tried property investing and renovated a couple of houses for rental (with more practical partners and skilled contractors). But while I could see that property investing might work for some people, I did not care enough about the details to make it work for me, and it was certainly not passive income.

I tried other things.

My first husband was a boat skipper and scuba diving instructor, so we started a charter. With the variable costs of fuel, the vagaries of New Zealand weather — and our divorce — it didn't last long!

From all these experiments, I learned I wanted to run a business, but it needed to be online and not based on a physical location, physical premises, or other people.

That was 2006, around the time that blogging started taking off and it became possible to make a living online. I could see the potential and a year later, the iPhone and the Amazon Kindle launched, which became the basis of my business as an author.

(6) Boring, automatic saving and investing works best

Between 2007 and 2011, I contracted in Australia, where they have compulsory superannuation contributions, meaning you have to save and invest a percentage of your salary or self-employed income.

I'd never done that before, because I didn't understand it. I'd ploughed all my excess income into property or the business instead. But in Australia I didn't notice the money going out because it was automatic. I chose a particular fund and it auto-invested every month. The pot grew pretty fast since I didn't touch it, and years later, it's still growing.

I discovered the power of compound interest and time in the market, both of which are super boring. This type of investing is not a get rich quick scheme. It's a slow process of automatically putting money into boring investments and doing that month in, month out, year in, year out, automatically for decades while you get on with your life.

I still do this. I earn money as an author entrepreneur and I put a percentage of that into boring investments automatically every month. I also have a small amount which is for fun and higher risk investments, but mostly I'm a conservative, risk-averse investor planning ahead for the future.

This is not financial advice, so I'm not giving any specifics. I have a list of recommended money books at www.TheCreativePenn.com/moneybooks if you want to learn more.

Learning from the Shadow

When I look back, my Shadow side around money eventually drove me to learn more and resulted in a better outcome (so far!).

I was ashamed of being poor when I had to wear hand-me-down clothes at school. That drove a fear of not having any money, which partially explains my workaholism. I was embarrassed at Oxford because I didn't know how to behave in certain settings, and I wanted to be like the rich people I saw there.

I spent too much money in my early years as a consultant because I wanted to experience a "rich" life and didn't understand saving and investing would lead to better things in the future.

I invested too much in the wrong things because I didn't know myself well enough and I was trying to get rich quick so I could leave my job and 'be happy.'

But eventually, I discovered that I could grow my net worth with boring, long-term investments while doing a job I loved as an author entrepreneur.

My only regret is that I didn't discover this earlier and put a percentage of my income into investments as soon as I started work. It took several decades to get started, but at least I did (eventually) start.

My money story isn't over yet, and I keep learning new things, but hopefully my experience will help you reflect on your own and avoid the issue if it's still in Shadow.

Questions:

- Which of the statements about money in this chapter resonate with you?

- Which of these statements and words trigger you or make you angry or upset?

- What are your memories around money?

- What are your fears about money?

- What words do you use about money and rich people? Are those words you would like to use about yourself if you were in that situation?

- What does your family say about money? How are those attitudes reflected in your behaviour around money?

- What does your culture say about money? (Friends, education, religion, media?)

- What is your money story? Reflect upon how things have changed over time and what lessons you have learned so far.

- Are you financially educated? If not, why not? Why haven't you spent time learning about money? How might this impact your future?

- How do you push money away? How do you reject it?

- How could money be a good thing for you and your author career?

- How can you change your attitude towards money to be more positive and achieve your financial goals?

Resources:

- List of books about money, both practical aspects of making and investing money as well as money mindset — www.TheCreativePenn.com/moneybooks

- *Business for Authors: How to be an Author Entrepreneur* — Joanna Penn

- *How to Make a Living with Your Writing: Turn Your Words Into Multiple Streams of Income* — Joanna Penn

2.7 The Shadow in the physical body

In *The Picture of Dorian Gray* by Oscar Wilde, the young Dorian Gray gazes at a beautiful lifelike painting of himself and says,

> "This picture will remain always young. It will never be older than this particular day of June… If only it were the other way! If it were I who was to be always young, and the picture that was to grow old! For that—for that—I would give everything! Yes, there is nothing in the whole world I would not give! I would give my soul for that!"

Dorian lives hard, enjoying all kinds of pleasure before descending into depravity and violence. The painting in his attic ages and becomes grotesque, even as he remains youthful and handsome.

But the painting haunts him, and in the end, appalled at what he has become, Dorian slashes it to ribbons. He becomes his repressed Shadow, kept in the attic all that time. As he dies, his body reverts to its true form and the painting is restored to its original state.

While this story might be extreme in its example, many of us spend years ignoring the reality of our bodies, favouring the mind and intellectual pursuits.

But we are physical animals and as much as we like to think otherwise, our daily decisions eventually manifest in our bodies. I've certainly wrestled with this over the years, so perhaps it's true for you, too.

> *Note*: I don't have experience of physical trauma, serious injury, long-term illness, disability, or certain mental health conditions. Please see a professional for your situation as appropriate.

The consequences of pushing the physical body into the Shadow

Have you ever looked at a photo of your younger self and thought, *I was beautiful back then. I wasn't fat and ugly like I thought I was. Why did I think that of myself?*

This type of body distortion is common, played out through cycles of self-judgment and the battle to mould ourselves into whatever shape society thinks is appropriate at the time.

In my teens and early twenties, the ideal body was represented by model Kate Moss, the waif, the skinny blonde. But I was a "fairy heffalump," as I was once called, crashing down the stairs with my bag full of books. I didn't fit in at ballet or tap classes. I didn't have the body for that — or the coordination.

But that was okay because I loved learning and knowledge and books, and my happy place was sitting alone reading or studying.

I was praised for being a bookworm and later rewarded for my good grades with money, and also with food treats. If I was a good girl and did well at school, I could have 'bad' or 'naughty' food like chocolate or cake or other treats.

The harder I worked, the more rewards I could get. This

association persists for me today. If I work hard, if I'm good — then I get a treat, preferably something delicious and bad.

Even as I write this, I realise how ridiculous it is, but seriously, does anyone reward themselves with kale?!

My focus on the mind instead of the body started from an early age. I pushed any idea of 'play' into the Shadow. It felt lazy and a waste of time to spend hours having what some called 'fun,' when I could be reading, learning new things, or escaping into another world.

My brother was always the athlete, physically confident and good at skateboarding and basketball and later the martial art capoeira. He also has several degrees and is a multi-award-winning photographer and filmmaker, so clearly it's possible to manage both sides!

But I wasn't interested in play or exercise for fun or pleasure because developing my mind was more important — at least that's what I told myself.

At school, we were forced into doing team sports like netball and hockey, which I hated. I never enjoyed group exercise and although I enjoyed swimming when I was younger, once I hit puberty, my body wasn't streamlined anymore and I couldn't swim so well. I didn't like to take my clothes off in the changing rooms, as I felt fat.

But that was okay because my body was just a vessel to carry around my mind, and my brain was the far more important aspect of my life.

I pushed physical health and fitness into the Shadow as unimportant, but the more you push things down, the more they come roaring back, eventually.

I started working in a global consulting company in 1997 and while I went to the gym — because that's what everyone did — it was the late nineties, a time of massive corporate expense accounts, and a work hard / play hard culture.

One of my first projects was in Brussels, Belgium, and most nights we were out at bars and restaurants having a *very* good time. During the day, my focus was on doing a good job and learning how to be an effective consultant, so it didn't matter that I put on ten kilos from moules-frites, binge drinking, and Guylian chocolate on the Eurostar home every week.

Consulting life burned me out, and I resigned in the year 2000 on my twenty-fifth birthday. I went traveling in Australia and eventually settled back into consulting as an IT contractor — and an office job once more.

I discovered scuba diving and became a PADI Divemaster so I could guide others underwater safely. I enjoyed the gym and took up running and cycling. I was relatively physically active and have continued to be — but I still prioritised my mind and my job over my body and spent most of the day as a sedentary computer worker.

As I hit my mid-thirties, I started getting back and shoulder pain. By the time we returned to the UK in 2011, I had such bad back pain that I had trouble sleeping. I had scans for spinal tumours, but they found nothing, and I was discharged for physiotherapy.

More years went by and I continued to go to the gym, as well as taking up yoga and long-distance walking. Despite all that, in 2019, I ended up with a shoulder injury that left me in agony.

When I couldn't lift my arm over my head anymore and almost passed out in the shower from the pain of trying to wash my hair, I went to a shoulder specialist.

He gave me a painkilling injection in my shoulder and a serious talking to, for which I am incredibly grateful.

He told me that my shoulder injury was from years of bad posture. Decades of hunching over a book, a desk, and a computer had wrenched my scapular out of position and unless I fixed my posture, I would be back in his office getting regular injections for the pain. They would eventually stop working and I would probably need an operation at some point. My pain would get worse.

The other option was to get serious and correct my posture, which I could do through weight training.

If you think I'm an outlier, or if you're young enough not to have significant pain yet, read *Deskbound: Standing Up to a Sitting World* by Dr Kelly Starrett. It notes that, "The typical seated office worker has more musculoskeletal injuries than any other industry sector worker, including construction, metal industry, and transportation workers."

I found a rehab gym and met Dan Clarke, who is still my personal trainer years later. We work out twice a week and I'm now proud to be a strong woman with healthy shoulders. My personal best dead lift is eighty-five kilograms at the time of writing, significantly more than my body weight. More importantly, I'm functionally strong and flexible and I have no persistent pain, just the normal sensation of muscles being used.

In working with Dan, I continue to learn body knowledge that I didn't value earlier in my life and which I now recognise as something I pushed away as unimportant for too long. I spend money and time on my physical health and I prioritise it over other things. I also love lifting, and it makes me feel fantastic.

Sometimes I get angry there were no role models of female strength when I was growing up, as I wish I had found lifting at a younger age. I was taught at school that the only exercise worth doing was team sports and I have never been a team player.

Strength was never seen as feminine and women with muscles were ridiculed for being overly masculine. I'm sure in some ways, they still are, but at least the body positivity movement has made different body types more acceptable. As tennis legend Serena Williams said, "Since I don't look like every other girl, it takes a while to be okay with that. To be different. But different is good."

It's complicated

While self-acceptance and self-love and self-care and body positivity are important and I absolutely agree that we should love our bodies and who we are right now, it's also complicated.

Your body and the state of your physical and mental health impact your quality of life now and for the rest of your days. Our brains are not separate from our bodies. We cannot keep prioritising the mind over everything else.

Clearly there are some conditions that are beyond your control, but wrestling with the Shadow around what we eat and how we move and how we treat our bodies and our minds is work many of us urgently need to do.

You only have to look at the headlines to see our Collective Shadow playing out. High rates of obesity, even in children. Eating disorders, binge eating, mental health issues, over-use of painkillers, medicalisation of so many conditions — and the list goes on.

If we don't do this work and figure out how our dysfunction is affecting our health, at some point, we will be forced into it. The pain will get to be too much. The Shadow will eventually rise up.

The Healthy Writer

In 2017, I co-wrote *The Healthy Writer* with Dr Euan Lawson. As part of the research for that book, we did a survey to see what authors suffered from.

It was shocking to discover how much pain there was in the community, with over 1,100 writers struggling with stress, back pain, weight gain, anxiety and sleep problems, as well as issues from sedentary working. Others reported headaches, eye strain, loneliness and depression, digestive issues, and repetitive strain injury.

It's clear that I'm not the only person who has pushed care of the physical body into the Shadow.

This is the work of a lifetime.

We live in our bodies and as the days go by, new challenges emerge. We may figure one thing out only to be greeted by something new.

In 2017, when *The Healthy Writer* was published, I had not experienced that chronic shoulder injury, and I had not discovered the joys of lifting.

I had also not reached perimenopause, which was a significant time for me, as it is for many other women.

In my midlife memoir *Pilgrimage*, published in 2023, I wrote about my physical and mental health struggles and some of the unexpected impacts of hormonal changes, as well as how COVID left me weak and struggling for months. While I was reticent to talk about such things at first, the process of writing about it brought it out of my Shadow, and I've heard from others that my words helped them in a difficult time.

These days, I'm happy to be lifting and walking and physically well, but I certainly haven't banished negative thoughts about what I look like in the mirror. I still feel fat and ugly some days. I still compare my body to other women and feel inferior. I'm still weak and in pain and broken some days. I still reward myself with food, and I have days when I eat way too much, or drink too much wine. I am a work in progress!

But I also know that the state of my physical body impacts my brain and my ability to write and create.

I cannot be an effective author and run a successful business without my health. I understand how much better I feel mentally when I move. I walk almost every day. I lift weights twice a week. Most days, I eat within a certain window based on the principles of intermittent fasting. I'm writing this at my standing desk.

I am not a saint by any means. I love my food — and I still love a drink! — but my denial of the importance of my physical body is over. As Hippocrates said, "Health is the greatest of human blessings."

Questions:

- What triggered you in this chapter?

- How do you feel about your body and your health?

- What words and phrases and images come up for you when you think about body image and health and how it has been portrayed amongst your family and your culture?

- How might you have pushed aspects of your body and health into the Shadow?

- In what ways could better physical health impact your creativity and your life?

- How might you address some of these issues in order to positively change your health?

- If you have experienced or are currently living with physical trauma, injury, serious long-term illness, disability, or mental health conditions, what are some of the potential Shadow aspects for you in terms of the way you see yourself, or the way others see you?

Resources:

- *Built to Move: The 10 Essential Habits To Help You Move Freely and Live Fully* — Kelly Starrett and Juliet Starrett

- *Deskbound: Standing Up to a Sitting World* — Kelly Starrett

- *The Body Keeps the Score: Brain, Mind, and Body in the Healing of Trauma* — Bessel A. van der Kolk

- *The Healthy Writer: Reduce Your Pain, Improve Your Health, and Build a Writing Career for the Long Term* — Joanna Penn and Dr Euan Lawson

"WHATEVER PAIN
YOU CAN'T GET RID
OF, *make it your creative
offering.*"

SUSAN CAIN

2.8 The Collective Shadow in country, society, and culture

> "Civilisation is like a thin layer of ice upon a deep ocean of chaos and darkness."
>
> —*Werner Herzog*

Some elements of our Shadow come from family, friends, and the choices we make in our lives. But other elements stem from our culture and the country we're raised in, as well as common aspects of human nature that lie within us all in what Carl Jung called the 'collective unconscious.'

He explained, "The collective unconscious contains the whole spiritual heritage of mankind's evolution born anew in the brain structure of every individual."

It also persists in the stories we tell; as Jung said, "the whole of mythology could be taken as a sort of projection of the collective unconscious."

The collective Shadow can therefore emerge when certain tendencies, behaviours, or traits are commonly denied, suppressed, or disavowed at a societal level. It may manifest through projection, especially when extreme views are taken on either side of the spectrum, forcing the opposite into Shadow.

When nuance and balance are lost, the Shadow emerges.

Where can you see that happening in your culture?

Uncovering the Collective Shadow

> "Wherever they burn books, in the end
> they will also burn human beings."
>
> —Heinrich Heine, *Almansor*

This is a vast area and ripe for misunderstanding, so rather than identifying specific things and triggering everyone, here is a list of questions to consider around your culture and your country.

Hopefully, they will spark thoughts and ideas about where aspects of the Collective Shadow lie and you can form your own questions to investigate further.

- Why might a society burn books? What does the content of those books tell you about the Collective Shadow?

- When a country is split between two major political parties, how might the extremism of one push the other even further?

- How might the Collective Shadow emerge through mob behaviour on social media? How did that occur during the pandemic? How did it affect you — and do you think differently now than you did at the time?

- When a country — or a group of people — think their customs or beliefs are superior, how might that spill over into imposing their values on others, in ways that range from critical comments to invasion and oppression?

- When a country's self-definition has been based on exceptionalism and the might of Empire, how might the Shadow emerge in modern times when equality and equity are demanded by those who were once considered inferior?

- When a religion forces restrictive sexuality at the same time as valuing hierarchy and patriarchy, how might the Shadow express itself in sexual dysfunction, denial, shame, and abuses of power?

- When a culture has valued one race — or class — over another for generations while building wealth and privilege for themselves, how might aspects of the Shadow eventually erupt and disrupt the status quo?

- When healthy forms of masculinity and aggression are oppressed by society, how might the Shadow side emerge?

- When a culture is founded on the principles of religious faith and the primacy of men, how might that impact modern attitudes to women's rights and bodily autonomy, as well as sexuality, and even innocuous behaviours like swearing?

Recognise the Collective Shadow in triggers

"The tendency to see one's shadow 'out there' in one's neighbour or in another race or culture is the most dangerous aspect of the modern psyche."

—Robert A. Johnson, *Owning Your Own Shadow*

Here are some words and phrases to consider:

Capitalism, socialism, conservatism, liberalism, patriotism, globalisation, open borders, immigration, universal basic income (UBI), universal healthcare, democracy, feminism, drugs, military strength, racism, billionaires, climate change, assisted suicide, gender identity.

These simple words and phrases are loaded with conflicting beliefs and misunderstandings. However you feel about each topic, try to consider what aspects of it may be part of the Collective Shadow.

Are there topics you respond to instinctively without considering the possible nuance?

What other words and issues spark controversy in your culture and/or country?

Importantly, **the Shadow is not the opposite of what you consider right**.

It lies in judgment, fear, anger, violence, or the demonisation of the Other.

If we can reflect on why we are triggered, and then question our immediate knee-jerk reaction, we can explore why we respond in this way, and expose deeper aspects of ourselves and our culture. In this way, we bring the Collective Shadow into the light and can choose whether we want to keep responding this way in the future.

Look for the nuance

If you don't want to be controlled by the Collective Shadow, then identify nuance rather than polarising issues.

Take the example of going to war.

Your personal and cultural experiences shape your initial thoughts. Here are some other possible opinions:

- War is always wrong. I'm a pacifist.

- I'm proud to serve my country and my family has always been proud to serve. We're patriots and if war is necessary, I will fight.

- Drones killed my family. The invaders called it collateral damage. I will go to war to defend my country and my home.

- I will go to war to stop the killing of innocents, even if the aggressor does not directly threaten my country.

- It's okay if *people* fight in wars, but autonomous drones and/or AI-powered weapons should be banned.

- It's not war if no one is physically hurt. Cyber-war, or war between robots and AIs, is better than the annihilation of human life.

If you consider different perspectives, even if you don't agree with them, you can discover nuance in any situation. This is the gift of story, either through fiction or personal experience in memoir and other non-fiction. We can portray different perspectives and hopefully encourage empathy across the divide.

There is polarity in every spectrum, but there is also nuance.

There may be black and white opinions, but there are also shades of grey in the Shadow.

The Collective Shadow is a rich vein for authors and artists

Many of the greatest books and films and TV shows use aspects of the Collective Shadow. They resonate because they strike a chord in people and evoke complex feelings on every side of a debate.

The Handmaid's Tale by Margaret Atwood reflects a dystopian view of gender roles and a totalitarian patriarchal state.

To Kill a Mockingbird by Harper Lee demonstrates the injustice of racism in the USA.

White Teeth by Zadie Smith illuminates the complex legacy of British imperialism through intertwined families in post-war London.

Brave New World by Aldous Huxley questions where technology might take us and what we might give up for perpetual drug-enabled happiness.

These are not essays or lectures on contentious subjects. They are fictional stories that explore themes and bring nuance through a variety of characters. This may be the most powerful and effective way to bring the Collective Shadow to light.

How the Shadow in my city helped me call it home

Evidence of the Collective Shadow can also be found in physical places.

Every country, every city, every town, every home has a

Shadow. Even if you remove the humans, nature is "red in tooth and claw," as Tennyson wrote.

Wherever you live in the world, you will find a Shadow if you go looking, and that may be where you find a well-spring of story.

At the time of writing, I live in the UNESCO World Heritage City of Bath, England, famous for its ancient Roman archaeology and hot springs, and eighteenth-century Georgian architecture. It's a beautiful place visited by tourists from all over the world and you might have seen it featured in the sweeping exterior shots of *Bridgerton*, *Persuasion*, and other period dramas.

I went to school in Bristol, the closest big city. I came to Bath for school trips back in the '80s, visiting the two-thousand-year-old Roman baths, but never considered it somewhere I might live.

When Jonathan and I moved out of London in 2015, we visited Bath as part of a decision-making process on where to live next. We also visited Edinburgh and considered York, cities with the dense history and architectural and cultural riches I missed while living in Australia and New Zealand for more than a decade.

On the weekend we visited Bath, it was the Jane Austen festival, all bonnets and simpering women with parasols parading around the gardens arm-in-arm with their gentlemen. I couldn't bear the faux-romance and the longing for another time that was terrible for women. It felt fake and contrived and I hated it.

(Yes, I know Jane Austen triggers me! Make of that what you will.)

And yet, something made me want to dig deeper. Surely a city with such a long history could not be all rainbows and unicorns. As Jung said, "How can I be substantial if I do not cast a shadow? I must have a dark side also if I am to be whole."

If it's true for an individual, then it must be true for a city or a country.

I first glimpsed that Shadow on the facade of the medieval abbey next to the Roman Baths. It features a stone carving of Jacob's Ladder on either side of the main arched window with angels climbing towards heaven.

Except one angel crawls *down*.

What sparked the desire to include what might even be a demon on the most prominent part of the abbey?

Perhaps the same human drive that caused ancient Romans to throw curse tablets into the hot springs, a place consecrated to a pagan goddess before it was ever Roman. These inscribed metal sheets call for the gods to punish evil-doers and bring down catastrophe on hated rivals in love and business.

There is more darkness in the city. Mary Shelley wrote *Frankenstein* here, a fact that Jane Austen fans like to ignore, although the two — very different — literary museums now lie only doors apart.

You can find elements of Freemasonry and the influence of druids in the geometric layout of the streets. There is a pagan god with a huge phallus in the Botanical Gardens, and there are ghost signs around the city, evidence of the long dead.

These things enabled me to catch a glimpse of the Shadow side of Bath and I could finally see myself living here. I am a flawed human, and I couldn't imagine living somewhere painted as so perfect and romantic, but I could see myself making a home somewhere with a dark side.

Since moving here, I've used the complexity of the city and its Shadow in my books.

In *Map of Shadows*, Sienna Farren inherits an antique map shop in Bath from her grandfather after he's mysteriously murdered. When she moves to the city, she discovers her heritage as a Blood Cartographer and must join the Mapwalker team to cross over into a world off the edge of our maps and prevent a coming war with the Shadow Cartographers.

I didn't consciously understand when I wrote the books that I was trying to make my home in Bath and find meaning beyond just a place to live. But I can look at the Mapwalker trilogy now and see how it reflects aspects of my journey in Sienna's search for belonging.

Take a deeper look at the place you live and notice how elements of the Shadow might inspire your writing.

Can we escape the impact of the Collective Shadow?

Sometimes individual humans are swept away by forces greater than anything they can control.

Much has been written about the Collective Shadow of Nazi Germany and the Holocaust. Did individual Germans from different backgrounds try to stop what was happening? Yes, of course, many did. But the Collective Shadow and the power of the mob were too great to stop what happened.

In my lifetime, there have been other atrocities that individuals could not stop due to regional and international conflicts — disease, famine, and climate-related issues amongst others.

Sometimes it feels like we are nothing on the face of the earth, that our lives matter so little in the grand scheme of things, and that we have no power in these situations.

But as Robert A. Johnson said in *Owning Your Own Shadow*, "Any repair of our fractured world must start with individuals who have the insight and courage to own their own shadow."

This is not about shame or guilt, but a greater awareness and responsibility. It is by making the darkness conscious that we can address our behaviour and then we might make a difference to those around us.

Questions:

- What traits, behaviours, or values does your culture proudly identify with? What potential Shadow might those traits conceal?

- What are the taboos in your culture and society?

- What kinds of people are marginalised or scape-goated or even demonised?

- What bias, prejudice, or systemic injustice exists in your society?

- What elements of your history or society get glossed over, idealised, or rationalised away?

- What addictions, self-destructive behaviours, or social dysfunctions are widespread in your culture? Why might that be?

- Are there books or movies or TV shows you feel illuminate aspects of the Collective Shadow?

- Where is the Shadow in the place you live, or have lived in the past?

- Are there ways in which you've written about aspects of the Collective Shadow? How might you bring facets into your work to give it more depth?

Resources:

- Druids, Freemasons and Frankenstein: The Darker Side of Bath, England — www.booksandtravel.page/bath-england/

- *Map of Shadows* and the Mapwalker trilogy by J.F. Penn — www.jfpennbooks.com/collections/mapwalker-dark-fantasy-thrillers

- *In Memoriam* — Alfred, Lord Tennyson

- *Owning Your Own Shadow: Understanding the Dark Side of the Psyche* — Robert A. Johnson

- *The Archetypes and the Collective Unconscious* — C.G. Jung

- *Psychology and Alchemy* — C.G. Jung

2.9 The Shadow in family and relationships

> "If you think you're enlightened,
> spend a week with your family."
>
> —*Ram Dass*

Just as every person has a Shadow, so every family has a Shadow, and sometimes it echoes back through generations.

It doesn't have to be caused by violence, trauma or abuse, neglect or shameful secrets, although of course, many suffer those things. Even if you had a happy, safe, and loving childhood, you still have a family Shadow, although perhaps it is more difficult to identify.

Examples of the Shadow in family

One of the most powerful and in-depth modern explorations of family Shadow is the TV series *Succession*.

Ageing media mogul Logan Roy needs to appoint a successor to his empire. He has four children from two separate marriages, each of whom is desperate for his love and hungry for his approval, while also being terrified of his anger. They fear being cast out, stripped of his love as well as their money and status.

Logan has his own traumatic past, overcoming poverty in working class Scotland to become a powerful billionaire with a direct line to the US president. In one scene, Logan is shown swimming, his back criss-crossed with deep scars. He fears death, rejecting advancing age and decline, clinging to power, while his children battle for his attention.

The series is powerful because it explores every aspect of family relationships: parents and children, each sibling to one another, partners and spouses, and even extended family issues. Love, hate, duty, guilt, rage, shame, fear. All laid bare in cutting dialogue that, at times, is more shockingly violent than a physical blow between people who ostensibly love each other.

Many Shakespearean tragedies centre around the Shadow of family. King Lear's desperate need for love from his three daughters leads to betrayal and madness. Romeo and Juliet are forced to hide their love from their warring families, which only ends in multiple deaths on both sides. Hamlet seeks revenge for his father's murder by his uncle.

Family conflict also echoes through myth and history, much of which is portrayed in art. I use paintings and sculpture as symbolic motifs in most of my fiction, and I struggled to decide which to use as an example here.

I settled on a dramatic example that remains seared into my mind: Francisco Goya's painting of *Saturn Devouring His Son*, which shows the wild-eyed titan consuming a bloody, decapitated corpse.

It stems from the Greek myth in which Saturn, also known as Kronos, heard a prophecy that he would be overthrown and murdered by one of his children, so he devoured each child at birth to prevent his own destruction. His wife eventually hides one of the children, Jupiter (also known as Zeus). Once grown, he indeed supplants his father just as had been prophesied, and indeed, it is a truth of humanity that the child must at some point surpass the parent.

You can see the painting in the Museo del Prado in Madrid, but Goya originally made it as one of the Black Paintings he created on the walls of his house between 1820 and 1823, amongst other religious and occult images. Goya certainly knew how to tap into Shadow for his art.

There are many other potential aspects of Shadow in human relationships. Consider your parents, siblings, extended family, partner or spouse, children, as well as extended family, friends, teachers, mentors, or other people who intersect with your life now or in the past.

Given how personal the Shadow is, perhaps it is best explored through art. As George Bernard Shaw said, "If you cannot get rid of the family skeleton, you may as well make it dance."

The Shadow in divorce

My first husband Richard left me for another woman — a slim, tattooed, scuba diving instructor who was happy to live on a boat and travel round the world working on yachts with him. They are still together many years later and I wish them all the best — at least I do now.

But the Shadow is not about other people. It's about how we react to events and process them for ourselves.

I didn't see anything coming until the day Richard told me he was leaving, and the years afterward were filled with Shadow for me.

I am so stupid. How could I not know something was wrong?

I'm not a good enough wife.

I'm not sexy or attractive or slim enough.

I'm not fun enough.

I'm not enough. Perhaps I never will be.

I wrote as a way to make the darkness visible and externalised my rage and hurt into words. I filled journal after journal with emotional poetry and reams of scrawled anger and misery. I didn't talk to a therapist because the blank page was my way forward and out.

Eventually, writing helped me figure out my part in the end of our marriage, because there were two people involved and blaming Richard didn't help me move forward.

I'm ferociously independent, but the Shadow side of that is the tendency to try and control everything. I need a partner who will communicate and tell me to stop rather than let me steamroll away while resentment festers inside, eventually erupting into an explosion from seemingly nowhere.

I'm grateful to Richard because the failure of our marriage helped me learn and grow and incorporate lessons into my relationship with Jonathan. I'm writing this chapter on our fifteenth wedding anniversary, so it's definitely going better the second time around!

Of course, there's no guarantee of the future, but I know the time I spent making the unconscious conscious about my mistakes helped me become a better partner.

> "Knowing your own darkness is the best method for dealing with the darknesses of other people."
>
> —C.G. Jung

Questions:

I've used 'family' here, but you can switch that out for any other word to explore the Shadow in relationships.

- What do you hide from your family? What do you not want them to know?

- What are you guilty about? What have you lied about?

- What are you ashamed of?

- What fears do you have around family?

- What duties do you perform for your family?

- What role do you play in the family when members are gathered together? What patterns do you fall into?

- Do you feel abandoned or rejected by your family?

- Where is the conflict in your family and who is it between?

- Is there competition for love or attention? Do you notice favouritism or inequality?

- As much as you hate to admit it, how are you similar to your parents? What flaws can you see in them, and are they mirrored in you?

- Where is the dysfunction in your family history? Can you see echoes further back to your grandparents or other family members? How can you break the pattern?

- How is your life now controlled by aspects of family? What do you resent? What are you angry about? Where is the repression in your family relationships?

- How can you move forward in a more positive way?

2.10 The Shadow in religion

"The forbidden object becomes dangerous and revered."

—Connie Zweig, *Meeting the Shadow of Spirituality*

I stood in the packed church, surrounded by the faithful as they lifted their arms to heaven and spoke in tongues. As the band played on, the pastor prayed aloud, calling for those who would commit their lives to Jesus to come forward.

It was 1990. I was fifteen and in a turmoil of hormones and angst, desperate to belong to something bigger than myself. The soaring music and mass emotional power of the event swept me away, and I went to the front of the church to accept Jesus into my heart. The community laid hands upon me as they prayed, their eyes full of acceptance, and I was welcomed in.

I was particularly drawn to the idea of a Father God who loved me as his special child. My parents had divorced years before and in those teenage years, I saw my dad occasionally but we weren't close, as we are now (love you, Dad!), so I sought love and approval from a father figure. The evangelical church gave me that through the image of Father God and also through the strong male leadership in the church, who I still remember as kind and good men.

Religious faith was a haven for me, but it was also a rebellion. My dad was raised as a Jehovah's Witness and rejected it in his teenage years, along with all religious faith. My mum embraced much of what the church called 'new age.' Neither were religious, so the church was a place I could be a different person away from the expectations of family and school.

I'm so grateful for those years. I was part of an energetic youth group, with holiday camps combining outdoor activity and education around faith. I loved singing along with the band and helping out at church in the youth group. I took a year out before university and worked in a Christian community outreach program, taking assemblies and classes in schools, and helping run youth groups and holiday camps. I even went on a mission to Berlin and also worked for a Christian charity at a school near Bethlehem.

My various teenage boyfriends were Christian, and our physical behaviour was constrained by the strength of our faith. We often prayed together, rather than indulging in the usual things teenagers get up to. Probably for the best!

But my faith was built on a fragile base of heightened emotion fuelled by evangelical fervour. When I started a degree in theology at the University of Oxford, my faith began to crumble under the rigour of intellectual examination.

But it was the Shadow that finally finished it.

My church taught that sex before marriage was a sin. The physical, animal act was held up as something pure and holy and dedicated to God. It should only be done after committing to someone for life in marriage — and, of course, that person had to be of the opposite sex. God loves the sinner but hates the sin, as they used to say about all kinds of things, including homosexuality. I began to question everything I was taught and whether I wanted to be part of a church that had views I didn't agree with.

My doubts crystallised in 1994 when the serial killer Jeffrey Dahmer was baptised and became a Christian in prison. He had been convicted of the murder and dismemberment of seventeen men and boys, and those stark words hide the horror of what he did to their bodies before and after death. The man was everything we might consider to be evil.

I still remember the sermon at my church when the pastor praised Jesus that this man had asked forgiveness and come to God. According to the gospel, he had been forgiven. Christ had died for his sins, as much as he had died for mine.

Later that year, Dahmer was beaten to death in prison by another inmate, and according to my church, because he repented, he was now in Heaven.

At the same time I was told — as a nineteen-year-old at that point — that if I had sex before marriage, I would go to hell unless I repented and changed my ways. They also said that the kind Muslim family down the road would go to Hell, and that the friendly lesbian police officer who used to be a lodger in our house would go to Hell, too.

But Jeffrey Dahmer would go to Heaven.

That's the day I lost my faith. I didn't want to be associated with a God whose idea of justice I could not agree with.

Of course, I know now that Christianity is not one thing, faith is not one thing, and God is not organised religion.

Every religion — and ideology and political party and worldview — has its own way of including insiders and banishing the Other.

God — or the Universe, or whatever you believe — is surely

above such petty human matters. But at the time, my faith was vested in these flawed people who told me things had to be a certain way.

I gave up on my evangelical faith.

I had sex a few months later and really enjoyed it. Perhaps my rebellion against the church made it even better. Sex had been pushed into the Shadow for too long and so I indulged with enthusiasm!

A new religious convert is often over-enthusiastic and proselytises in the first flush of faith. Losing a religion can be equally as galvanising, but eventually both settle into equilibrium. The emotions may dissipate, but the questions remain.

I have a master's degree in theology. I specialised in the psychology of religion and wrote my thesis on why people perform evil acts because "God told them to do it." But I am not a Christian.

I do not believe that Jesus Christ was the Son of God and died to save us from our sins. I will not recite the Apostle's Creed. I don't believe in a personal Father God who cares about me individually.

However, I believe there is more than just this physical world.

I experience moments of spirituality, mainly in nature or in places of deep historical faith, like cathedrals, where beauty brings me closer to whatever universal spirit ties us all together. I wrote about some of these in my memoir *Pilgrimage* and will keep exploring these connections through the voices of my fictional characters.

Religion also continues to be a creative muse. Almost all my books contain questions of faith, supernatural elements related to demons or angels, and places that resonate with religion and its dark side. The bones and blood of religious relics, ecclesiastical facades depicting the torture of saints and sinners, the persecution of the Other, secrets kept in the Vatican archives — all these things fascinate me and appear in my stories.

The Bible is full of dark things — a vengeful God who dashes the heads of babies on rocks, asks a father to kill his beloved son, and arranges the destruction of all who stand against him; incest and murder and rape; the destruction of cities; betrayal and hate of other tribes.

The cross of Christ is an instrument of torture and murder, and the Catholic crucifix has the tortured body of a man hanging there, blood pouring from his wounds. The Bible — and the history of faith — is full of the Shadow of humanity, and that is why it continues to inspire my stories and those of countless others.

The Shadow in rejecting or leaving a religious tradition

Religious faith can be your strength and solace, the centre of your community, and an integral part of your life. But there is a problem with making a religion out to be perfect, and holding the people who run places of worship up to be somehow incapable of darkness.

What happens when you question the 'truth' espoused by leaders of your faith community?

Perhaps you still have faith in God, but not in those who

claim authority in the name of religion? How do you manage your disillusionment?

If you leave your religious community, what impact does that have on your family, friends, and community?

One of the greatest human fears is to be cast out of the tribe, alone in the wilderness. Ending a relationship with a religious group can result in ostracism and grief, which may be pushed into the Shadow and emerge later in life.

"Sadly but inevitably, the longing for the light typically evokes its opposite: a shattering encounter with spiritual darkness, an emptying out of hope, meaning, and previous images of god. Our suffering hollows us out, tears at veils of spiritual persona, smashes religious idols, and ultimately leaves us bereft."

—Connie Zweig, *Meeting the Shadow of Spirituality*

Questions:

- What is your personal history with religion and faith?

- How has that shaped who you are today?

- Do you have guilt or shame associated with religion or aspects of faith? Examine why that might be and whether it's something you can bring out of the Shadow.

- Do you judge yourself? Do you judge others? How does that relate to your religious history and tradition?

Resources:

- List of books I love, many with religious or occult elements — www.jfpenn.com/bookrecommendations

- *Meeting The Shadow of Spirituality: The Hidden Power of Darkness on the Path* — Connie Zweig

- *Pilgrimage: Lessons Learned from Solo Walking Three Ancient Ways* — J.F. Penn

"AT MIDLIFE,
I met my devils."

CONNIE ZWEIG

2.11 The Shadow in midlife and ageing

If we're lucky to live long enough, there are some experiences we will all go through. There is no escaping them, and they will bring both challenges and gifts, Shadow and gold.

Much of the writing that resonates with us stems from these places, and our experience of them can inspire our deepest work.

The Shadow in midlife

"In the middle of the road of my life I awoke in a dark wood where the true way was wholly lost."

—*Dante Alighieri*

We spend the first half of our lives constructing a persona that is acceptable to our partner, family, friends, our faith, culture, and society. But as we reach a midway point, we start to question whether that's how we want to keep living.

To revisit Robert Bly's metaphor in *A Little Book on the Human Shadow*, we spend the first half of our lives stuffing aspects of ourselves into a bag that we drag behind us and then spend the rest of our lives trying to get them out again.

At midlife, there may be a clash between who we've built ourselves into, who we feel we truly are, and who we want to become. It might be a realisation of needs and desires we've denied and repressed. It can be a time of grief as past roles become less important, your body changes, and you feel a loss of purpose.

<u>At midlife, the Shadow demands attention.</u>

Owning and accepting it gives us a chance to make conscious choices about how to live the second half of life in a different way.

But that doesn't make the journey any easier.

How I met the Shadow in midlife

"At midlife I met my devils."

—Connie Zweig, *Meeting the Shadow*

I stopped sleeping properly in November 2019. I could fall asleep at first but would wake in the early hours and not be able to sleep again. I tried meditation and all kinds of natural supplements, and I read books about different ways to beat insomnia. When the pandemic started soon afterward, I blamed my sleeplessness and misery on anxiety.

The lockdowns took their toll. My mood darkened.

I often went to bed in the afternoon. I wasn't able to work and didn't want to. Some days, I cried for no reason. I was angry and frustrated, then empty and blank. Everything felt pointless.

On one particularly dark day, I stared down into the swirling waters of the flooded river and thought about sinking to the bottom. I've written about this time in *Pilgrimage*, but suffice to say, it was difficult.

One reality of being a woman in midlife is the menopause, although some women go through it earlier, and we all experience it in different ways. Once I realised that many of my symptoms were hormonal, I made some changes.

Going on hormone replacement therapy (HRT) helped me sleep and reduced other uncomfortable physical symptoms, while also helping my mental health. I know HRT is not for everyone, but it has been life-changing for me. If you or anyone you love is going through menopause, then I recommend reading *Menopausing* by Davina McCall.

Menopause also brings a psychological shift. It's an animal thing, completely out of your control. Your body changes and you cannot hold back time as each day ticks by.

It's also a visceral realisation of ageing.

I grieved for the young woman I had been and everything she represented. Perhaps I'm still grieving.

I took so much for granted, and when it's lost for good, there is an inevitable impact on how you perceive yourself. There is so much to say here, but I'm not through it yet.

I'm reading lots of books on midlife experience. I'm finding Connie Zweig's book *The Inner Work of Age* helpful as she writes of facing your inner ageist, "that part of you that rejects yourself by hanging onto youth, self-image, success, control, and denial of death at all costs."

I spent years pushing midlife and ageing into the Shadow, pretending it wasn't happening, almost denying it would happen to me. When symptoms of perimenopause hit, I spent more than a year without even considering that hormonal change might be the issue. I literally did not even imagine the possibility I was entering menopause. That was for older women, not me.

When I finally accepted the possibility, I could address it, and I'm slowly accepting what that means in other ways, some more metaphorical and meaningful than others.

Older women have not been served well by stories and myths, or the media. While older men are considered the elder statesman, the silver fox, or the distinguished gentleman, older women have been called the crone, the hag, and sometimes — thankfully — the wise woman.

In her book *Hagitude*, Sharon Blackie uses the metaphor of alchemical transformation for the experience of menopause, equating it to stages in psychological transformation. She notes that "the substance that is transforming suffers deeply, and it's forced to shed superfluities so that its true nature can be revealed… The goal during this initial phase of transformation is to reduce the individual down to her bare essence, to strip her down to her most essential parts."

It is here we face the Shadow and the difficult emotions we have pushed down or refused to face, the parts of our life that we no longer fit into, our conformity to roles imposed by others, the parts we can now burn away.

I love how Blackie talks of the fire that burns us during menopause — the night sweats, the hot flushes, the rage. She says its function is "to burn away the dead parts of our lives so that we can reveal the buried treasure within."

In reading the words of other women, I've found a path forward and am slowly pivoting into what the second half of my life will look like, with a much greater sensitivity to what truly matters.

Your experience will differ to mine, but acceptance of the inevitability is perhaps the first step for us all.

Ageing

There is much we can do to have a healthy, happy old age, but there are also many potential challenges.

If we push aspects of ageing into the Shadow so we don't have to face reality, at some point, they will rear up regardless.

Denial of age and its impact on the body may lead to avoidance of doctor's appointments and check-ups, or overly aggressive corrective procedures for cosmetic reasons. It may result in unhappiness with how your older body looks and feels.

Pain and decreased mobility, as well as recognizing a limit on what is possible in the time left, can lead to bitterness and irritation with self and others. There may be regrets around past mistakes or feelings of failure, sadness at choices not made, or disappointment at dreams unfulfilled.

There may be grief at the loss of loved ones and anger at the damage done by those closest to us. There might be a different kind of grief at the loss of identity and a difficulty in accepting that society — and perhaps even our family — sees us in a way that we cannot reconcile ourselves to.

As Connie Zweig says in *The Inner Work of Age*, "This is the last line of the song."

What will we sing in those last notes?

I write this from the perspective of a healthy forty-eight-year-old in the process of uncovering what is in my own Shadow around old age. Frankly, I'm terrified of what could happen if I'm lucky enough to make it that far.

My highest value is freedom, and independence defines my life. From a young age, I was encouraged to be self-sufficient, to be my own knight in shining armour. To make my own money, to never ask for charity, to never need help from others.

To be considered useless, lazy, stupid, and a burden are the worst things I could be accused of. They are the essence of my Shadow and the things I struggle to integrate. Who am I if I cannot work? Who am I if my brain starts to atrophy and I lose my independence?

Statistically speaking, I am likely to end up on my own. Jonathan is a few years older and men usually die earlier than women, plus we are (happily) childfree. So, I save and invest for the future, to make sure that I can look after myself in old age since it's unlikely there will be decent government support by the time my generation gets to retirement age.

But of course, there is much gold to be found in the Shadow and many gifts of old age, if we can accept them: The perspective of years of life and the wisdom that comes from experience. The rewards of helping family and friends and enjoying the maturation of relationships. The ability to mentor others and help those on the same path towards new insights. Time to spend on personal growth, creative pursuits, and new adventures in the world with a loving partner, friends, or happily alone. The appreciation of small things, and the ability to live in the moment.

Years ago, a wise older friend told me, "Just wait until you don't care what other people think anymore. That will be the most powerful time for you creatively."

I couldn't understand what she meant back then — how could I ever get to the point of not caring what other people think? But now, I'm starting to glimpse who that person might be, and she is empowered by what has previously been kept in the Shadow of ageing.

Connie Zweig, in *The Inner Work of Age*, recommends moving "through the passage of late life as a rite, releasing past forms, facing the unknown, and emerging renewed as an Elder filled with vitality and purpose."

That is what I'm trying to move towards, and this book marks another step in the journey. Perhaps I will write another memoir when I've figured out the next chapter — or perhaps I will read yours.

Questions:

- What feelings, thoughts, and words come up for you around midlife and ageing? Include aspects of your physical body as well as career, family, mental health, money, and anything else that comes up.

- What are you resisting in this area?

- What 'devils' did you meet at midlife?

- Are there ways you can achieve what you want to in the second half of life? How can you reframe the experience?

- How do you feel about old age? Where does the Shadow lie there for you?

Resources:

- *Hagitude: Reimagining the Second Half of Life* — Sharon Blackie

- *Menopausing: The Positive Roadmap to Your Second Spring* — Davina McCall

- *Midlife and the Great Unknown: Finding Courage and Clarity Through Poetry* — David Whyte

- *The Gift of Aging: Growing Older with Purpose, Planning and Positivity* — Marcy Cottrell Houle

- *The Inner Work of Age: Shifting from Role to Soul* — Connie Zweig

2.12 The Shadow in dying and death

> "The meaning of life is that it stops."
>
> —*Franz Kafka*

We all die.

It's an inescapable truth that every single person will face death in their lifetime. We will have to experience the death of others and the resulting grief, and ultimately, our own end.

We will also vicariously face it many times through books, TV, movies, and gaming since it is often the pivot point of story.

But death itself is not the Shadow.

As David Richo writes in *Shadow Dance*, "Death is not the shadow of life but its necessary counterpart, an ingredient, a season of the cycle by which nature thrives and renews itself."

It is our feelings and behaviour and attitudes about death that reveal the Shadow, both individually and in our culture, religion, and society.

I've always had an awareness of death. I don't know why. It's just always been there.

I have a black skull bracelet in front of me as I write and a brightly coloured sugar skull covered in butterflies on the shelf behind me. I like to visit graveyards and ossuaries and catacombs filled with bones, contemplating the truth of 'memento mori' — remember, you will die. Much of this interest emerges in my fiction, and I have several episodes about it on my Books and Travel Podcast with places to visit if you are of a similar mind.

In 2022, I had an artist's mark made for my J.F. Penn brand. It's a decorative sugar skull with my initials entwined within. I use it within my books as well as on my websites. It helps me keep 'memento mori' in mind as I write, since every book is a choice in how to spend the limited time I have left.

Some might consider these interests morbid, but they help me live more fully, knowing that the end will come at some point. I know my life is finite, and that helps me focus on making the most of it.

I used to think that other creatives would feel something similar, as so much of writing and story is based around death, but that turns out not to be true.

Here are some ways that death remains in the Shadow.

Denial

I made my first will in my thirties when I bought my first house. I like being organised and I never want to be a burden to my family, so over the years, I've done all the necessary paperwork, including power of attorney documents in case of dementia or head injury.

Perhaps my pragmatism comes from my mum as she has already paid in advance for her funeral and leaves a sheaf of papers on her desk when she goes on holiday with directions for everything, just in case she doesn't return.

So it's fascinating to me how many people die without a legal will or an estate management plan, especially if they are creatively and financially successful. This refusal to engage with what happens after death can leave much damage in its wake, presumably stemming from the denial that death would ever come.

When Stieg Larsson, who wrote *The Girl with the Dragon Tattoo*, amongst other books, died in 2004, he did not have a will. Legally, his extensive estate went to his father and brother, rather than his partner of thirty-two years.

Pablo Picasso died aged ninety-one without a will. It took six years and over $30 million to settle his estate between six heirs. Prince, Jimi Hendrix, Aretha Franklin, and Bob Marley are other examples.

But they are not unusual.

In the USA, LegalZoom reports that only 32 percent of Americans have a will.

Today's Will and Probate in the UK reports that fewer than four in ten adults in the UK have a will.

Common reasons people put it off are that it feels morbid earlier in life, or that they don't want to talk about it and cause conflict in the family while they are still alive. Perhaps they don't know how to make a will, or what the ramifications are if they don't have one. Maybe they think they don't have anything valuable enough to make it worthwhile.

But it all comes down to avoidance and denial of the inevitable.

Fear

Even though death is inevitable, some fight it with every breath they have.

It might be through avoidance of the topic in conversation or through behaviour like missing health checks and scans. It might be the denial inherent in extreme risk-taking behaviour, while almost courting death.

It could go in the other direction and involve an obsession with health, taking endless supplements or following different drug regimes and dietary practices to stave off death. You can see this in the tech billionaires obsessed with longevity by injecting stem cells and younger blood and investing in research that may just keep them alive long enough to live forever.

Fear of death can also be seen in attempts to control what happens after death, an obsession with legacy through complicated inheritance structures.

Or it can emerge in attempts to control the experience of death, which I recognise in myself.

I want the right to die, pain-free, when I choose. I support the charity Dignity in Dying, which campaigns for assisted dying for terminally ill patients, enabling access to quality end-of-life care and choice over how and when to die.

I recognise the hubris in trying to control death, but there is some comfort in preparing for a possible future, even while the end is far more likely to come from some unexpected direction.

Suicide

> "The key is in accepting your thoughts,
> all of them, even the bad ones."
>
> —Matt Haig, *Reasons to Stay Alive*

Note: If you need help in this area, please contact a suicide prevention service in your country. In the US, go to 988lifeline.org, and in the UK, go to www.samaritans.org.

I first read Thomas Hardy's *Jude the Obscure* as a teenager. It shaped my desire to go to Oxford, Jude's Christminster, and it was also the first time I remember encountering suicide. In the book, it is practicality, a misguided act of love to help others. It is understandable.

In my crime thriller *Delirium*, Lyssa, the sister of one character, died by suicide before the book begins and her death echoes through the story.

In one scene, her brother Matt says, "Some days it's a surprise that we continue to live. It's much harder to keep getting up and living in this world than it is to give up and relax into the darkness. Embracing oblivion is just a choice."

I also wrote Lyssa's diary for her. One excerpt reads:

> "What if this blackness is part of me, not separate. What if it's bound into every atom of my body? When they try to rip it from me, or sedate it, or electroshock it away, they're destroying all of me. I am every colour on the spectrum and I need black to highlight the

bright yellow, and iridescent green, and to let my brilliant turquoise shine. Without black, there is no contrast. Without contrast, life is monochrome."

I've shared further thoughts in the Author's Note at the back of *Delirium*, and in *Pilgrimage*, and I've talked openly about death on both my podcasts over the years. I'm grateful that I haven't been shamed for sharing my experience, or felt judged. In fact, people have told me it's helped them feel more normal about their thoughts. Suicide is not in my Shadow, but it remains there for many others.

Most people will know someone who has been affected by suicide, or have a family member or friend who has decided to die that way. It is certainly not unusual to think about it.

The mental health charity Mind notes that "one in five people have suicidal thoughts… Women are more likely to have suicidal thoughts and make suicide attempts, but men are three times more likely to take their own life than women."

This is clearly a common human experience, but by pushing the idea of suicide into our collective cultural Shadow through shame, guilt, or denial, we make it much harder for people to ask for help. It's better to have it out in the light and talk about it, even though it's difficult, and in that way, hope to prevent possible tragedy.

"Revealing my darkness is just as
natural as revealing my light."

—baek sehee, *i want to die but i want to eat tteokbokki*

Grief

Psychiatrist Elisabeth Kübler-Ross first outlined five stages of grief in the 1960s and that has since been expanded to seven. People may experience different stages at different times, or skip stages, or find themselves repeating aspects of each.

The stages are shock and denial, pain and guilt, anger and bargaining, depression, then the upward turn, reconstruction and working through, and finally, acceptance and hope. Of course, there are no exact 'rules' for grief. The stages are not linear and they may not happen in this order.

Max Porter writes in *Grief Is the Thing with Feathers*, "Moving on, as a concept, is for stupid people, because any sensible person knows grief is a long-term project. I refuse to rush. The pain that is thrust upon us let no man slow or speed or fix."

The framework goes some way to normalising such a universal human experience, and the Shadow arises when we push elements of the process away as inappropriate or shameful or wrong, or we're told we're not allowed to feel that way. For example, our guilt at not having done more while someone is alive may compound if not acknowledged as normal, or we may struggle when being told to just get on with life when we need more time.

The experience of collective grief became clear for many of us during the pandemic. Shock and denial in the early months, the thought that it would all be over soon and we could just muscle through. Anger that erupted online and onto the streets. Bargaining around behaviour to avoid illness, and judgment of those who got sick. Guilt around not doing more for others, or condemning people for thinking differently or behaving in ways we considered wrong. Depression for many and eventually, a realisation that life would not go back to how it had been.

In a *Harvard Business Review* article in March 2020, grief specialist David Kessler noted, "We feel the world has changed, and it has… The loss of normalcy; the fear of economic toll; the loss of connection. This is hitting us and we're grieving. Collectively. We are not used to this kind of collective grief in the air… We are grieving on a micro and macro level."

Cultural attitudes to death and dying

Death is dealt with differently in every culture. Some handle it in a healthy way out in the open, while others push it into Shadow.

I'm English and our way of grieving is possibly one of the most unhealthy, underscored by a 'stiff upper lip' and an attitude of restraint. The dead body is kept hidden. At a funeral, quiet crying is allowed but certainly no loud wailing at the graveside. Any out-of-control emotion is frowned upon. We stay silent, speak in whispers, shy away from discussing death. We use the excuse that we are giving people space to grieve, but perhaps we just don't know how to talk about it.

In other cultures, death is far more accepted and even celebrated. The body may be laid out in an open coffin for family and friends to visit a last time. There might be keening and ululating, a death wail to honour the dead, to comfort those grieving and as a cathartic release of pain. There might be a wake, a celebration of life.

In Varanasi, India, the burning ghats turn bodies to bone dust and ashes day and night on open pyres covered in marigolds.

In Tibet, sky burial leaves the corpse decomposing on a mountain top, exposed to the elements and eaten by wild animals.

In Mexico, Day of the Dead celebrates death and honours the ancestors. People dress in skeleton-themed costume, feast at the graveside, and acknowledge death by eating sugar skulls.

Established rituals around death can help the living with a structured approach to the end. This can be both a comfort to the person dying so they know how things will be managed, and a consolation to those left behind. It's one less thing to think about in the administration involved after death.

Perhaps those of us who live in cultures that avoid death, and those of us untethered from religious tradition, need to spend time considering what death might look like for us, and for those left behind. In this way, we can bring death out of the Shadow and into the light of awareness, removing its power to control our unconscious behaviour and preparing for what will come.

> "All that lives must die, passing
> through nature to eternity."
>
> —William Shakespeare, *Hamlet*

Questions:

- What are your feelings about death and dying?

- What are the personal and cultural experiences that have shaped your attitude?

- Do you have a will and/or estate management plan? If not, why not?

- In what ways do you recognise fear of death and dying in other people's behaviour, speech, or attitudes?

- Can you recognise any of these in yourself?

- What are your thoughts about suicide? What are the cultural and religious attitudes around it and how might that push suicidal thoughts into Shadow?

- How have you experienced grief? How does it affect you? Are there ways you can accept the stages of grief for yourself or for others?

- What are your cultural or religious practices around death?

- How can you bring aspects of dying and death out of the Shadow and into the light of awareness?

Resources:

- Suicide prevention services: www.988lifeline.org (USA), www.samaritans.org (UK)

- *Grief Is the Thing with Feathers* — Max Porter

- *i want to die but i want to eat tteokbokki* — baek sehee

- *Reasons to Stay Alive* — Matt Haig

- *Shadow Dance: Liberating the Power & Creativity of Your Dark Side* — David Richo

- *Smoke Gets in Your Eyes: And Other Lessons from the Crematorium* — Caitlin Doughty

- *The Author Estate Handbook: How to Organize Your Affairs and Leave a Legacy* — M.L. Ronn

- Memento Mori: How Travel Can Help Us Deal with Death and Grief with Dr Karen Wyatt — www.booksandtravel.page/grief-death-travel/

- Life Obsessed: Cemeteries, Graveyards, and Ossuaries with Loren Rhoads — www.booksandtravel.page/cemeteries-graveyards/

- Dignity in Dying — www.dignityindying.org.uk

- LegalZoom Estate planning statistics — www.legalzoom.com/articles/estate-planning-statistics

- Today's Will and Probate UK — www.todayswillsandprobate.co.uk/only-4-in-10-uk-adults-have-a-will-despite-owning-a-property/

- Mind mental health charity — www.mind.org.uk

- Seven Stages of Grief —
  www.choosingtherapy.com/7-stages-of-grief/

- List of books about grief —
  www.choosingtherapy.com/grief-books/

- "That Discomfort You're Feeling Is Grief," Scott
  Berinato, *Harvard Business Review*, March 23, 2020
  — www.hbr.org/2020/03/that-discomfort-youre-
  feeling-is-grief

- "The Men Who Want to Live Forever," Dara Horn,
  New York Times, January 25, 2018 —
  www.nytimes.com/2018/01/25/opinion/sunday/
  silicon-valley-immortality.html

MEMENTO MORI

Remember, you will die.

Part 3:
Turn Your
Inner Darkness
into Words

3.1 Open the doors

In *The Dark Side of the Light Chasers*, Debbie Ford uses a metaphor of a castle to explore the idea that we all have hidden and repressed parts of ourselves. The castle has a thousand unique rooms, some beautiful, some strange, others exotic, or scary. Each has a precious gift within.

As a child, you ran freely through all those rooms, playing in every one, curious about what you might find. Expanding your horizons.

But over the years, you closed certain doors because of criticism, rejection, judgment. For some, these doors might have been closed through violence, or trauma.

You closed other doors because the rooms weren't appropriate in your society, culture, or family, and still more through shame, embarrassment, and fear. You locked the precious gifts away.

But what if you could roam your castle freely once more?

What if you could open the doors covered in cobwebs that you have avoided for so long?

What if those precious gifts remain inside and you might rediscover them, and use them to create your most important work?

Perhaps you've already glimpsed some long-ignored rooms you might want to explore during the previous sections of this book. Perhaps ideas are forming as to how you can bring aspects of your Shadow into the light and incorporate them into your writing.

This final section takes the journey further to help you open the doors into the rest of your castle, mine the precious gold in your Shadow, and share it in your books.

Questions:

- Imagine your castle with all its rooms. Which doors did you close and why?

- Which doors would you like to open again?

- Which doors are you afraid of entering?

- What precious gifts might be hidden inside?

Resource:

- *The Dark Side of the Light Chasers: Reclaiming Your Power, Creativity, Brilliance, and Dreams* — Debbie Ford

3.2 Accept who you are

"The most terrifying thing is to accept oneself completely."

—C.G. Jung, *Psychology and Alchemy*

Who would we be without our Shadow side?

We cannot know as it's impossible to find out. You will never be perfect with no flaws. You cannot go through life without scars. You cannot avoid difficult, even damaging situations along the way.

The question is how you interpret them and how you use them in your life going forward.

Some people survive the worst atrocities and emerge transformed, spending their lives in service to humanity.

Others who go through the same thing spiral into behaviour that destroys themselves and other people.

Most of us sit somewhere in between these extremes. We do not suffer atrocities and we are not completely broken and unable to function in the world.

But we all have a Shadow side.

We hide it by wearing masks, by avoiding that which we are ashamed or afraid of.

So how can we stop hiding?

You are a mess — so am I

A lot of the time, we are not okay. We just pretend we are because we have to get on with all the things we have to do to live a functional life and be a responsible human.

We avoid engaging with the chaos, the broken side, the repressed Shadow. We put on a brave face and hide what's really going on.

Connie Zweig in *The Inner Work of Age* says, "We each have a flaw, a crack, a shadow. We are vessels with imperfections, wounds, and regrets… If we are fortunate, we can even begin to see the gifts of our wounds and the beauty of our cracks—and even the beauty in the cracks of others. We begin to see how our wounds gave us our uniqueness— how the light shines in through them."

Part of this process is accepting our cracks and flaws, and accepting the Shadow in ourselves and others. We're all a work in progress, so let's stop pretending otherwise.

As Brené Brown says in *The Gifts of Imperfection*, "Owning our story and loving ourselves through that process is the bravest thing that we'll ever do."

It's not about blaming others

"If someone comes along and shoots an arrow into your heart, it's fruitless to stand there and yell at the person. It would be much better to turn your attention to the fact that there's an arrow in your heart."

—Pema Chödrön, *Start Where You Are*

It's worth spending time on writing out all the hate and blame and anger and envy and guilt and fear — and everything else — you hold towards other people to explain why you are who you are today.

Spend some time really letting loose.

Be as self-indulgent and self-pitying as you can.

Maybe terrible things have happened to you and other people have caused you great pain. Whatever it is, write it down.

But once you've wallowed in that sticky, smelly mud for long enough, it's time to clamber out, wash it off, and get on with creating a new version of yourself.

How do you know when you've been wallowing long enough?

You will know because you'll be sick of feeling that way, and the pain will be enough to drive you to make a change.

Back when I was truly miserable in my day job as an IT consultant, I used to blame others for my situation. I couldn't work out how I ended up there doing a job I hated. It seemed like the result of more than a decade of unconscious choices shaped by the expectations of other people and society. I didn't know how to get out of the situation — but I was sure I could find the answer in a book.

In 2005, I read *The Success Principles: How to Get from Where You Are to Where You Want to Be* by Jack Canfield. The first principle is "Take 100% responsibility for your life."

The rest of the book is filled with useful advice, but that

principle in particular struck me hard. I could only change my life if I stopped blaming others, and took action towards my goals.

I started writing my first non-fiction book, which would become *Career Change*. In 2008, I started my website, TheCreativePenn.com, then my podcast, and then I started writing fiction. One step after the next.

In 2011, six years after reading *The Success Principles*, I left my consulting job to become a full-time author entrepreneur. I took responsibility for my life, and I never looked back.

You can't change other people. You can't change the past. You can only change yourself and forge a new path for your future.

It's not about removing the Shadow completely

This process is not about finding everything in your unconscious and getting rid of it all. It's about recognising aspects of your personality and then becoming more aware, so you can stop them from being in charge, and prevent them from sabotaging you in ways you can't control.

It's also about channeling some of those areas in a healthier way, sublimating them into our words, and using the richness of our hidden depths to deepen our creative body of work.

As Jung said, "One does not become enlightened by imagining figures of light, but by making the darkness conscious."

Of course, self-acceptance and self-love are not about just patting yourself on the back and saying, 'Well, great, I'm fine as I am,' and never improving.

It's about balance.

We can work towards accepting who we are right now — including our elements of Shadow — and still move forward, developing and growing and changing as we become a better version of ourselves.

This is the work of a lifetime

It's not like you will one day be a flawless being with no inner darkness.

You can't pull all the Shadow out, deal with it in one fell swoop, and be all shiny and perfect.

As we grow and change, additional aspects of Shadow emerge to be dealt with. We will also push new things into the darkness as we face fresh challenges at different stages in our lives.

It's not about fixing everything.

Kintsugi is the Japanese art of repairing broken pottery in a way that embraces the cracks, chips, and damaged parts rather than trying to hide them. Gold or silver is mixed with lacquer to highlight the lines and make the repair an integral part of the remade object. It's considered more beautiful *because* of its obvious flaws.

Writing is a safe way to explore and express your Shadow

Once again, I'm not suggesting you throw off the shackles of civilised society and start indulging everything your Shadow self would love to do.

If you act in those self-destructive ways, the Shadow has taken control and will drive you off a cliff.

But you are a writer.

You can put whatever the hell you want onto the blank page.

You can safely write your unedited self into your books and no one need know it's there. But you will know, and in that way, you can bring aspects of your Shadow safely into the light.

> "The artists… who touch us deeply are the ones who are not so scared and limited to only express their appropriate qualities. The ones we are moved by are the ones who are brave or eccentric enough to go to the edges of what's normal and safe."
>
> —Jamie Catto, *Insanely Gifted*

Questions:

- How are you a mess right now?

- What are the things about yourself that you struggle to accept?

- In what ways do you blame others for your situation?

- How can you take 100 percent responsibility for your life?

- How can you work towards accepting your cracks and flaws — or even making them a beautiful part of who you are?

Resources:

- *Insanely Gifted: Turn Your Demons into Creative Rocket Fuel* — Jamie Catto

- *Start Where You Are: A Guide to Compassionate Living* — Pema Chödrön

- *The Gifts of Imperfection: Let Go of Who You Think You're Supposed to Be and Embrace Who You Are* — Brené Brown

- *The Inner Work of Age: Shifting from Role to Soul* — Connie Zweig

- *The Success Principles: How to Get from Where You Are to Where You Want to Be* — Jack Canfield with Janet Switzer

"THE MOST TERRIFYING THING *is to accept oneself completely.*"

C. G. JUNG

3.3 Stop self-censoring

"I want to stand as close to the edge as I can without going over. Out on the edge you see all the kinds of things you can't see from the center… Big, undreamed-of things."

—Kurt Vonnegut, *Player Piano*

Self-censorship is a natural response to the pressures we face as writers and as humans in this increasingly noisy world. Every day we're bombarded by other people telling us what it's okay to think, and therefore to write.

Societal norms and expectations constrain us, news media headlines make us want to conform for fear of judgment, and social media rewards us by responding to the 'likes' of the crowd.

But when you censor your ideas before you have even written them, you are letting fear of judgment, fear of rejection, and fear of backlash from an imaginary audience stop you.

Your thoughts are nothing until you put them onto the page, and what emerges in writing is often completely different from what you thought it might be in your head.

If you censor yourself before you even get to the blank page, you may never discover the edge, or the "big, undreamed-of things" that Vonnegut spoke of. You may never find your gold.

Does your inner critic come from the Shadow?

You can't think that.

You can't write that.

You can't imagine those things.

Who do you think you are?

You don't have permission to write that, to think that, to publish that. To be that person.

We all have an inner critic, a voice that says we are not good enough, that an idea is terrible or has been written before, that our words are worthless. Perhaps the voice of your inner critic comes from something in the Shadow? As I recounted earlier in Chapter 2.2, it was the criticism of a teacher early in my life that made me think I couldn't write in a certain way.

So how do we stop self-censoring to write what we really want to? Here are some ideas.

(1) Don't tell anyone you're writing

If you write as if no one will ever read your words, you might be able to sidestep self-censorship.

Your creativity is a fragile seed at the beginning of every book, and even more so at the beginning of your author career. When the fresh green shoots emerge above the surface, they are easily bruised and broken, stamped upon by others, or can die from lack of care.

Sometimes it's best to keep your writing secret so you can

protect your little seedling until it is strong enough, with roots that go deep enough, to weather the treatment it will have to face. In this way, there are no expectations hanging over you, no pre-judgments restricting your growth.

(2) Change your physical location when writing

The places where you live and visit regularly become part of your routine. You also perform certain roles in your home or place of work.

If you want to break out of the expectations of those roles, then find a new place to write.

Break yourself out of your comfort zone.

Try a new coffee shop or write in your car overlooking a new setting, or sit at a new desk facing the opposite way at the library.

If you must be at home, change the atmosphere. Listen to a new playlist, sit somewhere different, or light a candle with an unusual scent. Anything to make the experience distinct enough from how you usually create.

(3) Write another book

I've found that the easiest way to deal with fear of judgment around a particular book is to write another. Partly because I grow more confident as an author with every book, so I'm more secure in my creative expression. Partly because the emotional attachment to a book, and how much we identify ourselves with it, lessens when focusing on a new project, and fades even further with the distance of time.

We change with every book we write.

We transform through our creative work and with each book, we can push our boundaries a little more.

Poet Stephanie Wytovich delved into this form of progress in an interview on The Creative Penn Podcast:

> "If we can find a way to acknowledge our lines, or acknowledge where we put our boundaries, and then start having conversations with ourselves about why those boundaries are there, what those boundaries are protecting us from, and then slowly start inching over them in our writing, I tend to think that that's where the gold usually lies."

(4) Surround yourself with people who understand

Let's face it, writers are weird!

We spend a lot of time in the strange corners of our imagination, musing about random ideas, talking to characters we made up. If you're like me, you might be blowing things up and killing people and creating mayhem and destruction — on the page, of course.

If you externalise these thoughts around the wrong people, they will judge you for it, and their reaction may shut you down.

It's a hard truth, but our family and friends — those who love us in our 'normal' life — are often the least interested in our books. They are not our ideal readers, as much as we think they should be interested, so let them be.

Instead, find a supportive community of like-minded weirdos, and your creativity will flourish.

Investigate communities around your genre. I'm a member of the International Thriller Writers and also the Horror Writers Association, and I find both to be full of welcoming writers who don't find me weird at all. Such a relief!

You can also find groups around your publishing choices. I'm a member of the Alliance of Independent Authors as well as the Society of Authors.

There are plenty of Facebook groups around genre-specific topics, and for writers at every stage of their career.

None of these are perfect. People are people, and groups and organisations also have their Shadow side, but if you spend some time actively looking, you will find a supportive community somewhere.

(5) Use a pseudonym

Pseudonyms, or an alias or fake name, have often been used to shield authors from judgment or prejudice, or to separate brands based on audience expectations.

Since women could not publish in the nineteenth century, the Brontë sisters published their first collection of poetry together under male names. Emily's *Wuthering Heights* and Charlotte's *Jane Eyre* were also originally published under male names.

Louisa May Alcott, author of the tame and societally acceptable *Little Women*, also published "blood and thunder tales," under A.M. Barnard. Stephanie Sylverne, in an article on CrimeReads, notes, "This was the work Alcott was passionate about before the financial needs of her family forced her into writing what she called 'moral pap for the young.'"

Using a different name can also help keep your writing self separate from you as an individual. It can give you a layer of protection to prevent people in your normal life associating you with your writing.

Authors who are also medical doctors, lawyers, police officers, and others have used pseudonyms to protect their professional reputation.

Many erotica authors use different names. For example, Erika Mitchell wrote *Fifty Shades of Grey* as E.L. James.

Writing under a pseudonym can also be a way to expand into other genres without impacting your existing reputation or confusing or offending your audience. It can help you escape the confines of an established brand and become more creatively free.

Mystery writer Agatha Christie wrote other types of novels under the name Mary Westmacott, exploring what one biographer called "her most private and precious imaginative garden," while she was best known for her more formulaic murder mysteries.

J.K. Rowling writes much darker crime novels as Robert Galbraith to escape the Harry Potter fantasy expectations of her original readers.

I write under two names, but it's been a complicated process.

My full name is Joanna Frances Penn, but family and friends have always called me Jo. When I started writing, I wanted a professional name, but I was told that many Americans considered 'Jo' to be a man's name, so I published under Joanna Penn.

I wrote several non-fiction books and my first couple of novels under Joanna Penn, but then I realised that this cross-genre writing was confusing to my readers and muddied my non-fiction brand.

Originally, I had everyone on the same email list, which was hard to manage, and it messed up the algorithm-driven, also-bought lists on the online retailers. In addition, I received several reviews from readers saying that they "were surprised a woman had written this," and I didn't want to be pre-judged for my gender.

So, I split out my fiction under J.F. Penn, and the use of gender-neutral initials is a common choice for authors. I've also found it helpful creatively as I'm a different writer as J.F. than I am as Joanna Penn. This book straddles both of my author personas, but it is at heart a self-help manual for writers, hence it's under Joanna Penn.

It's certainly more effort to run two author brands, but it's helped me to explore my Shadow and focus on distinct audiences. Only you can decide what's best for your creativity and your author career.

Questions:

- How do you self-censor? How do you stop yourself from writing what you really want to?

- What does your inner critic say about you and your writing?

- Where does your inner critic come from?

- How can you bypass your inner critic, especially while you're writing your first draft?

- If you had no constraints, no fear of what others might think, what would you write?

- How might things change if you wrote in secret?

- Where do you write at the moment? Is that place associated with a specific role or expectations that might be constraining you?

- How might writing in a new place liberate you?

- Do you have a community of like-minded creatives? If not, where might you find them?

- How might a pseudonym help you write what you really want to?

- What are the pros and cons of pseudonyms?

Resources:

- *Agatha Christie: A Mysterious Life —* Laura Thompson

- "Louisa May Alcott's Forgotten Thrillers are Revolutionary Examples of Early Feminism," Stephanie Sylverne, CrimeReads, November 22, 2019 — www.crimereads.com/louisa-may-alcotts-thrillers

- Writing Poetry in the Dark with Stephanie M. Wytovich — www.TheCreativePenn.com/wytovich

3.4 Strengthen your characters

In the words of Carl Jung, "How can I be substantial if I do not cast a shadow? I must have a dark side also if I am to be whole." In turn, if we are to make our characters whole and bring them to life on the page, we can use principles of Shadow to give them depth.

Our heroes cannot be all good, our villains cannot be all bad. They must have different facets to make them believable, and their complexity and human flaws will make them memorable in the minds of readers.

There are some classic literary characters that portray the Shadow side as a clear duality.

In the novella *The Strange Case of Dr Jekyll and Mr Hyde* by R.L. Stevenson, Dr Jekyll drinks a potion that splits his consciousness into two. It even changes his physical form. The evil Edward Hyde emerges to commit violence and murder, then all he has to do is drink another potion to turn himself back into the responsible and moral Dr Jekyll, who tries to atone for the sins of his darker half.

In a confessional letter, Jekyll writes of his nightly adventures as Hyde,

> "When I would come back from these excursions, I was often plunged into a kind of wonder at my vicarious depravity. This familiar that I called out of my own soul, and sent forth alone to do his good pleasure, was a being inherently malign and villainous; his

> every act and thought centred on self; drinking pleasure with bestial avidity… It was Hyde, after all, and Hyde alone that was guilty."

Perhaps we can all relate to times when we indulged in behaviour our responsible selves would condemn. I've certainly woken up more than once and wondered who the hell I was under the influence of a potion that tasted a lot like tequila. Thankfully, not for a long time!

We all have a drug of choice, and mine has always been alcohol. There's certainly no issue with a few glasses of wine with friends and family, or a few G&T sundowners. It's excess and being out of control that is the Shadow acting out.

Admitting and acknowledging this brings it out of the Shadow and into the light. While I was certainly ashamed of myself in the depths of those killer hangovers, I can look back now with the gifts of middle age and be grateful that I didn't do more damage to myself or others.

Back to the story. Jekyll understands that by indulging Hyde, he makes that side of him even stronger:

> "I began to spy a danger that, if this were much prolonged, the balance of my nature might be permanently overthrown, the power of voluntary change be forfeited, and the character of Edward Hyde be irrevocably mine… I was slowly losing hold of my original and better self."

In this way, Jekyll taps into a concept that Jung also expresses around the Shadow. The more we repress an aspect of ourselves, the more we push it down, the more violently it may explode at some other point in our lives. As Jekyll admits, "My devil had been long caged, he came out roaring."

In terms of modern literature, *Fight Club* by Chuck Palahniuk portrays an unnamed narrator who discovers a darker alter ego. Tyler Durden encourages him to engage in bare knuckle fist-fights, saying, "Maybe self-improvement isn't the answer… Maybe self-destruction is."

Both books portray characters who allow the Shadow side to take the reins, but for most of our stories, we do not need to split a character so exactly in two. The Shadow is less a binary construct and more a continuum that differs for every character.

"Some of the greatest and most compelling characters in literature are the villains and the psychos, all born from the darker, less acceptable realms of the writer. It is when the hero goes into the darkest part of the forest that he discovers the gold."

—Jamie Catto, *Insanely Gifted*

Character flaws

Characters who wrestle with their Shadow selves inevitably have flaws that make them far more relatable and human — and readers want to know what happens when those flaws drive a character to action.

Character flaws are aspects of personality that affect a person so much that it's the challenge of the story to face and overcome them.

In *Jaws* by Peter Benchley, the protagonist Martin Brody is afraid of the water, and he has to overcome that flaw to destroy the killer shark and save the town.

Breaking Bad is so compelling as a TV series because Walter White's journey from mild-mannered chemistry teacher to drug kingpin is all about his flaws and yet, despite the dark themes, the audience cares deeply for him and the other characters along the way.

Succession remains one of my favourite TV series. Logan Roy is flawed as a father and his children are so broken because of him, but familial love is complicated and the show demonstrates those very flaws in all their variety.

Some flaws are about personality. A character who values status above all else may marry someone who helps them ascend in the social hierarchy, but perhaps they can only find true love when they overcome that flaw.

Some flaws are more life-threatening. A character with an addiction to painkillers might lie to cover up spending patterns and spiral into debt to fund their need.

As with real people, never define your characters purely by their flaws.

The character addicted to painkillers might also be a brilliant and successful female lawyer who gets up at four a.m. to work out at the gym, likes '80s music, and volunteers at a local dog shelter on the weekends. There are plenty of functional addicts who don't fit the stereotype too often portrayed in the media.

Part of your job as a writer is to break out of cliché and write original, compelling characters, and sometimes we can only do that by seeing our own dark side.

"No matter what you see on the outside, everyone struggles on the inside. Everyone is damaged, some people more severely than others, and the hurts we've experienced in life leave wounds that change the way we view the world and ourselves. Sometimes flaws develop as we attempt to defend against further hurts."

—Angela Ackerman and Becca Puglisi,
The Negative Trait Thesaurus

Back story wounds

Elements of Shadow often originate in scars, wounds, trauma, and painful memories rooted in a character's past. Character wounds are formed from life experience and arise from events that happened before the story even begins, but they shape a character's reactions in the present.

Katniss Everdeen in *The Hunger Games* carries the wounds of a traumatic childhood shaped by poverty, the loss of her father, near starvation, and the burden of providing for her mother and sister in a violent and unequal society. These wounds shape her mistrust of others, her survival instinct, and the anger that feeds her Shadow as she navigates the brutal Hunger Games.

She needs these darker elements to survive, win the games by killing others, and ultimately to defeat the regime that oppresses her people. Katniss is not a loveable character and although there are moments of tenderness, her dark side remains ascendant, as it needs to be for the plot — and readers love her for it.

In my ARKANE thrillers, Morgan Sierra's husband Elian

died in her arms during a military operation before the series begins, but her memories of it recur when she faces a firefight, and she struggles to find happiness again for fear of losing someone she loves once more.

Of course, trauma affects people differently, and the variety of responses may provide even more dimensions to a story.

For example, the COVID pandemic was traumatic for many, but its impact on behaviour varies. For some, hand-washing and virus-avoidance practices turned into Obsessive Compulsive Disorder (OCD), and some struggle to leave the safety of their home. Some people have scarred lungs, others have scarred memories. Still others couldn't wait to get back out in the world and seek adventure once more.

Question your assumptions about where a wound came from and how it may affect your character.

The Shadow in the antagonist

The most straightforward manifestation of the Shadow is through the antagonist or villain. These characters often represent the darker aspects of the protagonist's personality — traits they might deny, suppress, or struggle with.

I love writing villains and usually have fun creating my antagonists, although I also try to make their desires understandable.

In my thriller *Crypt of Bone*, Milan Noble is a good-looking, charismatic CEO of a pharmaceutical company that funds global healthcare initiatives. He's a well-respected businessman who gives money to the arts and cultural institutions. Much of his work benefits humanity.

But his company has a secret wing that focuses on population control through eugenics and also psychological manipulation, culling those Milan does not think are worthy to live, in order to fulfil the prophecy from Revelation that "a fourth of the earth" would be killed in the last days. He also seeks supernatural power through his search for The Devil's Bible, intending to use an ancient curse to transform himself and those who follow him.

Milan's back story includes an abusive, occult-obsessed father, hinting at a generational Shadow passed down through the bloodline, and he re-enacts the sins of his father through dark sacrifice.

Yet Milan is conflicted by his deeds and keeps an underground collection of bonsai trees he has spent years cultivating. For every death, he hammers a nail into one precious tree in atonement.

In another of my thrillers, *Tree of Life*, I found inspiration for my antagonist in extreme climate activism, which is understandable and even encouraged in our society at the time of writing.

Aurelia dos Santos Fidalgo is heiress to a Brazilian mining empire and grew up on the edge of an open cast mine owned by her father, while her mother pined for the Amazon rainforest of her youth. Aurelia wants to purge the Earth of those who pollute and destroy, and the only way to save the world is to eliminate all human life.

Secrets and lies

The Shadow loves secrets because a character will find ways to hide it, and that may lead them to behave in ways they never would normally. It might start with one simple lie, but spiral into actions that swiftly run out of control.

From addiction to affairs, from gambling and money issues to eating disorders, when a secret finally makes its way out into the open, it can destroy a life, a community, or a society.

In *The Secret History* by Donna Tartt, a group of students try to keep their involvement in a murder secret, but it slowly erodes their lives.

In real life, Bernie Madoff kept his Ponzi scheme a secret for decades before it imploded in 2008, when it was revealed he had defrauded thousands of investors out of billions of dollars. He died in prison, while one of his sons died by suicide, the other from cancer, and many of those who gave him money struggled to live on what they had left.

I recommend watching the Netflix documentary *Madoff: The Monster of Wall Street*. It's an incredible account of the lengths people will go to keep a secret and how enormous lies can be perpetuated, even for decades, before inevitably crashing down.

Temptation and obsession

The Shadow may tempt characters towards risky behaviour, taboo desires, dangerous obsessions, or moral compromises that threaten to overpower their rational self-control.

Fifty Shades of Grey is a fascinating case study for the power of the Shadow. While fantasies of bondage and control may be common, they were hardly topics of mainstream discussion until *Fifty Shades* brought BDSM erotica out of the collective Shadow and onto daytime TV (in certain Western countries, at least).

But the book is not just about sex. It's also about power.

The respective character arcs are almost a reversal. Christian starts out as physically dominant and emotionally distant, but in the story, Ana eventually emerges as the one who binds Christian to her.

Perhaps what is more interesting than the book itself is the reaction to it and what that reveals about the Shadow for an individual, or a society.

Transformation through a character arc

Memorable characters are those who overcome their flaws and wounds, their Shadow side, and transform into a new version of themselves.

In *The Lord of the Rings*, Frodo must overcome his addiction to the ring and the temptation it offers to throw it into Mount Doom and save Middle Earth.

In the *Star Wars* movies, Anakin Skywalker descends into the dark side to become Darth Vader, but eventually gives his life to save his son when the Emperor tries to kill Luke, overcoming the Shadow that had ruled him.

Do your research

Humans are complicated, and people react in different ways to different situations. We all bring our history and emotional baggage along for the ride of life. Don't assume that someone else's reaction would be the same as yours.

Don't lean on stereotypes or clichés. Do your research.

Read non-fiction books for facts and memoirs for the experience of a situation, as well as fiction to see how others have written about it.

Watch documentaries about people who've suffered, and films that feature characters with whatever form of darkness you want to include.

Interview people, watch YouTube videos, or listen to podcast episodes for authentic details.

You can't produce your best writing without filling your creative well, so research the Shadow in all its facets, and dip into your own to bring your characters to life.

I recommend two books in particular around this topic: *The Emotional Wound Thesaurus: A Writer's Guide to Psychological Trauma* and *The Negative Trait Thesaurus: A Writer's Guide to Character Flaws*, both by Angela Ackerman and Becca Puglisi.

* * *

Once again, look after yourself if you choose to research darker things.

You don't need to read graphic descriptions of murder to write from the perspective of a murderer. I've written a lot of death in my books and I've never read anything in the true crime genre. I read supernatural horror but not slasher gore fiction, and I don't watch horror movies. My imagination — and my fear — are more than enough.

If you find yourself dwelling too much on the darkness, switch to something else. Go for a walk, preferably somewhere you can see people being normal and nature carrying on as if you don't exist. I like walking by the river or the canal, listening to the birdsong and watching ducks paddle along, or the herons fishing. These things will continue long after I'm dead and that grounds me back into real life.

Questions:

- Consider the story of Dr Jekyll and Mr Hyde. What 'devil' has been long caged for you? How has it come out roaring?

- What are some memorable characters from your favourite books? What aspects of the Shadow can you recognise in them?

- If you have already written stories of your own, can you do the same for your characters?

- What kinds of authentic and interesting flaws can you develop for your characters?

- Why are you attracted to those flaws in particular?

- How can you use back story wounds to deepen your characters? What are some ideas you could use in future stories?

- How can you use the Shadow as part of your antagonist, but without making it everything that defines them?

- How could you use secrets and lies in your stories?

- How could you use temptation and/or obsession in your books?

- How can you use the character's Shadow as part of their transformative arc?

Resources:

- How Character Flaws Shape Story with Will Storr — www.TheCreativePenn.com/willstorr

- *Insanely Gifted: Turn Your Demons into Creative Rocket Fuel* — Jamie Catto

- *The Emotional Wound Thesaurus: A Writer's Guide to Psychological Trauma* — Angela Ackerman and Becca Puglisi

- *The Negative Trait Thesaurus: A Writer's Guide to Character Flaws* — Angela Ackerman and Becca Puglisi

"WRITE WHAT DISTURBS YOU, WHAT YOU FEAR,

what you have not been willing to speak about."

NATALIE GOLDBERG

3.5 Deepen your themes

"Write what disturbs you, what you fear, what you have not been willing to speak about. Be willing to split open."

—Natalie Goldberg, *Wild Mind*

There are layers to every book.

Theme is what the story is *really* about. Not the surface events of the plot, but the underlying concepts or principles that you want to underscore.

My crime thriller *Desecration* opens with a murder in an anatomy museum and, on the surface, it's a detective story about the hunt for the killer. But that's just the plot. The theme is how the physical body defines us in life — and in death.

Some authors start with a theme in mind.

Some authors discover their theme after they've written the first draft or later during the editorial process.

Still others may never understand their theme consciously, but readers comment about things in reviews that reveal an underlying theme after all.

Regardless of how you get to it, your choice of theme says a great deal about you as an author. Over time, recurring themes are a clear aspect of your author voice, which you can further deepen with elements of Shadow.

Universal themes

Universal themes appeal to the greatest number of people because they are aspects of life we all recognise. Some examples include good versus evil, pursuing justice at all costs, or love in all its forms, which may include sacrificing everything, the transformative power of love, love across borders, or lost love and grief.

You can deepen a theme by including elements of Shadow.

The Shadow side of love can include jealousy, obsession, heartbreak, violence, and abuse of power.

In a good versus evil story, a superhero may leave collateral damage in their wake, destroying some people's lives even as they save others.

If a character pursues justice at all costs, they might achieve their goal but end up destroying their life and their family.

Consider your favourite books, movies, and TV shows. Try to discern their themes and how the author has layered these themes into the story along with elements of Shadow, then see how far you can incorporate such aspects in your stories.

How your choice of theme might echo elements of your Shadow

> "An artist can show things that other people are terrified of expressing."
>
> —*Louise Bourgeois*

We are all drawn to specific themes, and noticing what reoccurs in your books can help reveal elements of Shadow. It might take years to understand, but the signposts will be there.

My fiction often explores themes around questions of faith, religion, and spirituality, as well as sacrifice for family which echo back to my early experience outlined earlier. But I didn't realise where my themes came from until years after writing, so trust your unconscious to incorporate elements, regardless.

If you uncover themes that hold personal meaning, you can tap into this emotional energy even further, lending greater authenticity and depth to your author voice, which is what readers will return for again and again.

Use symbolism to underscore theme

Symbols and recurring motifs are ways to bring more depth to your writing. They are a shorthand for meaning, and the most powerful symbols are those that resonate across cultures and generations.

Some symbols may be obviously related to theme. My thriller *Crypt of Bone* (unsurprisingly) includes images of bones, skulls, skeletons, and other portrayals of death in different guises as part of a good versus evil theme.

In *Destroyer of Worlds*, I used elements of fire and flame, candles and pyres, to reflect the cycle of creation and destruction, all elements associated with Shiva Nataraja, the Hindu god who dances the cycle of time surrounded by flames, a key element of the story.

It can be easier to tap into the unconscious through symbols and metaphor, so it will be interesting for you to discover what emerges in your writing.

Questions:

- Why is theme so important for stories that resonate deeply?

- What themes can you identify in books, films, and TV shows you particularly love and resonate with?

- How do aspects of the Shadow emerge in these themes?

- What themes can you identify in your writing?

- Can you recognise elements of Shadow there?

- What symbols are used in the books, films, and TV shows you love?

- What symbolism do you use in your books?

- How can you deepen theme with symbolism?

Resources:

- *Wild Mind: Living the Writer's Life* — Natalie Goldberg

- *Writing Your Story's Theme: The Writer's Guide to Plotting Stories That Matter* — K.M. Weiland

3.6 Writing the Shadow into other genres

"Only those willing to risk going too
far can find out how far they can go."

—*T.S. Eliot*

While it might seem more obvious to write elements of Shadow into adult mainstream fiction, it can bring richness to other genres as well. Here are a few examples — if your genre is not covered, then consider how you might incorporate elements of Shadow there.

Children's books and fairy tales

The world is scary, and children go through some terrible things. It's not surprising that many of the best-loved children's stories have elements of Shadow.

Hansel and Gretel in the witch's cottage about to be eaten.

Snow White with the huntsman coming to cut out her heart and the wicked stepmother who sends her to sleep with a poisoned apple.

Peter Pan with its Shadow realm of pirates and dying fairies in a world where you never grow up.

The Little Mermaid, who trades her voice to the witch and walks in agony on land for love.

Willy Wonka's chocolate factory, where there's a sinister price for over-indulgence.

The darker side of these stories is the reason for their longevity.

One of my favourite books as a child was *Where the Wild Things Are* by Maurice Sendak. I wanted to join Max's imaginary journey to the land of Wild Things and "Let the wild rumpus start!" But that kind of behaviour was not appropriate for this quiet, introverted child, so I experienced it vicariously through the story.

Then there are the memorable films of childhood. I was born in 1975 and those of my era are likely still scarred by *Watership Down* (1978) and *Indiana Jones and the Temple of Doom* (1984). Yes, they really did let us watch a full-on bunny massacre and a human sacrifice where a man's heart is torn out of his chest!

> "A children's story that can only be enjoyed by children is not a good children's story in the slightest."
>
> —C.S. Lewis

Memoir

The best memoirs have a clear character arc. Memoir teacher Marion Roach calls it the "transcendent change," from discontent and despair, through trials and hard-won experience, to a final revelation when the individual can start a new chapter.

She explained in an interview on The Creative Penn Podcast, "We're not reading your book because of what you did… We're reading your book for what you did with it."

Wild by Cheryl Strayed follows her journey along 1,100

miles of the Pacific Crest Trail from the Mojave Desert through California and Oregon to Washington State.

Cheryl's life spiralled out of control following the death of her mother, a divorce, and a period of self-destructive behaviour, and she embarks on the trail with no hiking experience.

Along the way, she tests her limits, confronts her fears, and through the crucible of extreme physical hardship, faces her Shadow and emerges transformed.

At one point, she questions whether she should regret her past reckless behaviour, the drug use and the casual sex: "What if what made me do all those things everyone thought I shouldn't have done was what also had got me here?"

This is a moment when the Shadow is brought into the light, where shame and regret dissipate and she can integrate her past into a reinvented self.

If only we could all do the same.

Wild is a great book and a perfect example of a clear character arc in memoir. It's also a huge bestseller and resonates with readers because it's so heartfelt and honest about facing darkness.

"You'll need both sides of yourself — the beautiful and the beastly — to hold a reader's attention."

—*Mary Karr, The Art of Memoir*

Non-fiction

The world is full of boring non-fiction books on every topic.

Don't write those!

Bring your full humanity to every book and consider where the Shadow might be in whatever you're investigating.

The Big Short by Michael Lewis, which became a film of the same name, is about the 2008 global financial crisis and those who made a fortune out of betting against the US housing market. It illustrates the Shadow side of the American Dream — the greed, the hype, the desire for riches — and we cheer for its anti-heroes even as they make billions off those who refuse to see the crash coming.

Another example is *The Immortal Life of Henrietta Lacks* by Rebecca Skloot, which exposes scientific exploitation and racism lying beneath now hugely valuable cancer cell research.

Both of these books won multiple awards, spent weeks on the bestseller lists, and were made into award-winning films.

Questions:

- Consider your favourite books, films, and TV shows of whatever genre. Where can you find aspects of Shadow in the books that resonate deeply?

- How can you incorporate such elements in your books?

Resources:

- *The Big Short: Inside the Doomsday Machine* — Michael Lewis

- *The Immortal Life of Henrietta Lacks* — Rebecca Skloot

- *Where the Wild Things Are* — Maurice Sendak

- *Wild: A Journey from Lost to Found* — Cheryl Strayed

- Writing Your Transcendent Change: Memoir with Marion Roach Smith — www.TheCreativePenn.com/marion23

- Resources for Writing Memoir — www.TheCreativePenn.com/writing-memoir/

"THE GOLD
is in the dark."

C. G. JUNG

3.7 Turn your Shadow into gold

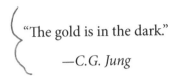

"The gold is in the dark."

—*C.G. Jung*

For the first thirty years of my life, I did not believe I was creative.

Perhaps it stems from that experience in my English class at school, or perhaps it was the overwhelming cultural message that a creative career would mean I'd end up a poor artist starving in a garret.

I like having money, and I always wanted to be financially independent and able to look after myself. I don't want to be a burden. So I pursued a career in business and pushed creativity into my Shadow, denying it was even part of me.

It was easier to do a job that ultimately I didn't care about than to face up to what I really wanted to do — a path that would open me up to criticism, judgment, and potential failure.

Steven Pressfield calls this a 'shadow career' in *Turning Pro*:

> "Sometimes, when we're terrified of embracing our true calling, we'll pursue a shadow calling instead… A shadow career entails no real risk. If we fail at a shadow career, the consequences are meaningless to us."

I worked in other people's businesses; I read other people's books, and spent my free time looking at other people's art in museums, galleries, and on cultural trips. I was obsessed with other people's creativity.

I'm grateful to my consulting job for making me so incredibly miserable that I was forced to eventually make a change.

In 2006, I wrote out an affirmation on a piece of yellow card: "I am creative, I am an author."

It wasn't true and I couldn't say it out loud, so I tucked the card into my wallet and recited the words in my head as I walked to the train station each day for my commute into the office.

One of the psychological tricks of affirmations is to create cognitive dissonance, an uncomfortable feeling that what you're saying is incorrect, so your brain seeks ways to fix it. You either have to take action to make it true, or you need to stop saying the affirmation.

That's when I began to work on what eventually became my first book, *Career Change*. I figured out ways to become more creative, to finally turn that affirmation into reality.

It took a few months before I could say "I am creative" out loud.

It took a few years before I published my first book and could say, "I am an author."

But in December 2008, I started my website, TheCreativePenn.com, because I could finally accept that I was indeed creative. Later, I started a company, The Creative Penn Limited, to further claim the word for my life.

In September 2011, I left my consulting job to become a full-time author and creative entrepreneur.

I've made a (very good) living from my words ever since.

My creativity lay in Shadow for so long, but I was able, over the process of years, to engage with it and slowly turn it into gold.

What is 'gold' for you?

Bringing creativity out of my Shadow has resulted in many kinds of 'gold.'

The most important one is that I feel my life has meaning and that I'm happy in my work as an author, exploring my ideas through my books and helping others. I measure my life by what I create.

It has also brought me friends and a community around the world, as well as a chance to develop myself and my craft and business skills. Then, of course, it has brought me financial reward, as I turn my creativity into books, products, and experiences that people want to buy — including this book!

The 'gold' in each aspect of your Shadow will be different, but it's important to consider as part of why it's worth delving into your darker side. If it's going to be a painful process, perhaps one that takes many years, what might the gold be on the other side?

Here are some possibilities.

(1) Readers will love your books

In 2022, Colleen Hoover dominated the bestseller charts.

The *New York Times* reported in October 2022 that she had sold 8.6 million print books already that year, more than James Patterson and John Grisham combined, and more than the Bible, with over 20 million sold over the course of her career. It was a fascinating article delving behind the scenes of Hoover's life.

Colleen self-published her first book in 2012 while making minimum wage as a social worker. Her husband worked as a long-distance truck driver, they had three sons, and the whole family lived in a small trailer.

Within six months, she had hit the *New York Times* bestseller list multiple times, made tens of thousands in sales, and quit her job to write full time.

I remember Colleen's books from the early days of self-publishing, but had never read one. Romance is not usually my preference, but like many people, I wondered how the hell she was so successful, and why readers were so in love with her stories. Social media and TikTok in particular might have fuelled the surge in her success, but even the best marketing cannot drive word of mouth and such fan adoration. Readers *love* Colleen Hoover's books!

I bought *It Ends With Us* and raced through it in two sittings. The first line reads, "As I sit here with one foot on either side of the ledge, looking down from twelve stories above the streets of Boston, I can't help but think about suicide."

The book is a dark romance, the love story of Lily Bloom and Ryle Kincaid, and features violence, domestic abuse, and the triumph of a survivor. Hoover was reported to have written it based on the relationship between her mother and father, describing it as "the hardest book I've ever written."

One of the most highlighted lines is this one: "There is no such thing as bad people. We're all just people who sometimes do bad things."

One fan on TikTok said, "I want Colleen Hoover to punch me in the face. That would hurt less than these books."

I think the success of Colleen's books is due to her ability to tap into the Shadow, and portray the incredible complexity of human nature in all its chaos and ugliness and beauty. She is real on the page and in her videos and her readers love her for it.

I don't mean we must all write about abuse or suffering, or romance, or the other tropes that she taps into.

We must be true to our own inner darkness.

We can learn all the writing craft techniques and all the marketing tactics, but books with heart — and Shadow — are the ones that readers love.

"Ultimately the product that any writer has to sell is not the subject being written about, but who he or she is."

—William Zinsser, *On Writing Well*

(2) You will learn more about yourself, about other people, and perhaps even heal your old wounds

"The only journey is the one within," as Rainer Maria Rilke wrote in *Letters to a Young Poet*. Measures of external success can be wonderful, but they're meaningless if you're unhappy with yourself and your life.

Perhaps the gold in your Shadow may help you overcome creative blocks, write more deeply, and live more authentically.

Perhaps it might be a realisation of a deeply held attitude that has shaped your life in an unconscious manner. By recognising it, you can decide to change.

Perhaps it might be a new appreciation of flawed loved ones, and an ability to feel empathy instead of anger or resentment.

Perhaps it is your ability to process whatever pain is in the depths of your creative soul, and finally let it dissolve onto the page.

By delving within, you will find your gold and it will differ from everyone else's. You will only know what it is when you find it.

(3) Your Shadow may help you navigate the way ahead

As previously explained, I write under two author names. Joanna Penn writes non-fiction self-help for authors — like this book. J.F. Penn writes thrillers, dark fantasy, crime, horror, short stories, and travel memoir — and maybe a whole load of other things in the future!

While I have plenty of books under each brand, I've spent 80 percent of my time over the last fifteen years focused on Joanna Penn. My white horse has been dominant.

I'm proud of what I've achieved and my books as Joanna Penn will hopefully continue to help people for many years to come. But I need to test the limits of what might be possible if I let my Shadow side out into my writing even more.

My travel memoir *Pilgrimage* written under J.F. Penn released me in so many ways and helped me write things I had previously kept hidden because I thought they were shameful or inappropriate. I was petrified about publishing it, because it felt like I was baring my dark little heart with all its bloody scars.

But *Pilgrimage* resonates with readers who seek what I did and the reviews demonstrate it touches people deeply as they recognise themselves in my experience.

I want to keep writing that way. I want the gold in my Shadow to be the seeds of my best creative work in the years ahead.

I want to let my dark horse run.

How about you?

> "Where we had thought to find an abomination, we shall find a god. And where we had thought to slay another, we shall slay ourselves. Where we had thought to travel outward, we will come to the center of our own existence. And where we had thought to be alone, we will be with all the world."
>
> —Joseph Campbell, *The Power of Myth*

Questions:

- What is 'gold' for you?

- How can you incorporate elements of Shadow into your life and creative work in the years ahead?

- How can you let your dark horse run?

Resources:

- "How Colleen Hoover Rose to Rule the Best-Seller List," Alexandra Alter, *New York Times*, October 9, 2022 — www.nytimes.com/2022/10/09/books/colleen-hoover.html

- *It Ends With Us* — Colleen Hoover

- It Ends With Us, Wikipedia page accessed 29 August 2023 — en.wikipedia.org/wiki/It_Ends_with_Us

- *On Writing Well: The Classic Guide to Writing Non-fiction* — William Zinsser

- *The Power of Myth* — Joseph Campbell and Bill Moyers

- *Turning Pro: Tap Your Inner Power and Create Your Life's Work* — Stephen Pressfield

Need more help?

Need accountability around writing the Shadow?

Several times a year, I run *The Shadow Sessions*, live online Zoom calls where you can join me and a group of other authors (although you're welcome to stay off-camera and anonymous) as I guide you through the process of Writing the Shadow.

Find out more at:

www.TheCreativePenn.com/shadowsessions

* * *

Need more help with writing and the business of being an author?

Sign up for my *free* Author Blueprint and email series, and receive useful information on writing, publishing, book marketing, and making a living with your writing:

www.TheCreativePenn.com/blueprint

You can find my books for authors in all formats on your favourite online store. You can also buy them direct from me at:

www.CreativePennBooks.com

* * *

Love podcasts?

Join me every Monday for The Creative Penn Podcast where I talk about writing, publishing, book marketing and the author business.

Available on your favourite podcast app.

Find the backlist episodes at:

www.TheCreativePenn.com/podcast

Selected Bibliography

Ackerman, Angela and Becca Puglisi. *The Emotional Wound Thesaurus: A Writer's Guide to Psychological Trauma*. JADD Publishing, 2017.

Ackerman, Angela and Becca Puglisi. *The Negative Trait Thesaurus: A Writer's Guide to Character Flaws*. JADD Publishing, 2013.

Anders, Charlie Jane. *Never Say You Can't Survive: How to Get Through Hard Times By Making Up Stories*. New York: Tor Books, 2021.

Blackie, Sharon. *Hagitude: Reimagining the Second Half of Life*. September Publishing, 2021.

Bly, Robert and William Booth. *A Little Book on the Human Shadow*. San Francisco: HarperOne, 1988.

Brown, Brené. *The Gifts of Imperfection: Let Go of Who You Think You're Supposed to Be and Embrace Who You Are*. Center City, MN: Hazelden, 2010.

Cain, Susan. *Bittersweet: How Sorrow and Longing Make Us Whole*. New York: Viking, 2019.

Cameron Julia. *The Artist's Way: A Spiritual Path to Higher Creativity*. New York: TarcherPerigee; Anniversary edition (2002).

Campbell, Joseph. *A Joseph Campbell Companion: Reflections on the Art of Living*. New York: Harper Perennial, 1991.

Campbell, Joseph. *The Power of Myth*. New York, NY: Doubleday, 1988.

Canfield, Jack, with Janet Switzer. *The Success Principles: How to Get from Where You Are to Where You Want to Be*. New York, NY: HarperCollins, 2005.

Catto, Jamie. *Insanely Gifted: Turn Your Demons into Creative Rocket Fuel*. Sounds True, 2016.

Chödrön Pema. *Start Where You Are: A Guide to Compassionate Living*. Boston & London: Shambhala Publications; Revised edition (2001).

Chödrön, Pema. *When Things Fall Apart: Heart Advice for Difficult Times*. Boston, MA: Shambhala Publications, 1997.

Elliott, Carolyn. *Existential Kink: Unmask Your Shadow and Embrace Your Power*. Weiser Books, 2020.

Ford, Debbie. *The Dark Side of the Light Chasers: Reclaiming Your Power, Creativity, Brilliance, and Dreams*. New York, NY: Riverhead Books, 1998.

Goldberg, Natalie. *Wild Mind: Living the Writer's Life*. New York, NY: Bantam Books, 1990.

Haig Matt. *Reasons to Stay Alive*. New York: Penguin Books; Reprint edition (2016).

Houle, Marcy Cottrell. *The Gift of Aging: Growing Older with Purpose, Planning and Positivity*. Cambridge: Cambridge UP, 2023.

Johnson, Robert A. *Owning Your Own Shadow: Understanding the Dark Side of the Psyche*. San Francisco: HarperOne, 1991.

Jung C.G. *The Archetypes and the Collective Unconscious*. Princeton University Press; Second edition (1969).

Jung, C.G. *Memories, Dreams, Reflections*. New York: Vintage Books USA, 1989.

Jung, C.G. *Modern Man in Search of a Soul*. New York: Harcourt Brace Jovanovich Inc., 1933.

Jung, C.G. *Psychology and Alchemy*. Princeton University Press; Reprint edition (1980).

Jung, C.G. *Psychology and Religion*. New Haven: Yale University Press; Second edition (1960).

Karr Mary. *The Art of Memoir*. New York : Harper Perennial; Reprint edition (2016).

McCall, Davina. *Menopausing: The Positive Roadmap to Your Second Spring*. London: Orion Spring, 2021.

Penn, J.F. *Pilgrimage: Lessons Learned from Solo Walking Three Ancient Ways*. Bath, UK: Curl Up Press, 2023.

Penn, Joanna. *The Successful Author Mindset: A Handbook for Surviving the Writer's Journey*. Bath, UK: Curl Up Press, 2016.

Pierce, Mark. *The Creative Wound: Heal Your Broken Art*. Independently published, 2019.

Porter, Max. *Grief Is the Thing with Feathers*. London: Faber & Faber, 2015.

Pressfield, Stephen. *Turning Pro: Tap Your Inner Power and Create Your Life's Work*. New York, NY: Black Irish Entertainment LLC, 2012.

Richo David. *Shadow Dance: Liberating the Power & Creativity of Your Dark Side*. New York: Shambhala; Revised edition (2003).

Sehee, Baek. *i want to die but i want to eat tteokbokki*. London: Bloomsbury, 2022.

Syme, Becca and Susan Bischoff. *Dear Writer, Are You Intuitive?*. Hummingbird Books, 2022.

Van der Kolk Bessel A. *The Body Keeps the Score: Brain Mind and Body in the Healing of Trauma*. Penguin Books; Reprint edition (2015).

Whyte, David. *Midlife and the Great Unknown: Finding Courage and Clarity Through Poetry*. New York: Riverhead Books, 2003.

Wright, David W. *Into The Darkness: Hook Your Readers (Without Getting Lost in the Dark)*. Sterling & Stone, 2019.

Zweig Connie. *Romancing the Shadow: A Guide to Soul Work for a Vital Authentic Life*. New York: Ballantine Books; Reprint edition (1999).

Zweig, Connie. *Meeting The Shadow of Spirituality: The Hidden Power of Darkness on the Path*. Nicolas-Hays Inc., 2003.

Zweig, Connie. *The Inner Work of Age: Shifting from Role to Soul*. New York, NY: Park Street Press, 2021.

More Books and Courses From Joanna Penn

You can find my books in all formats on your favourite online store. You can also buy them direct from me at:

www.CreativePennBooks.com

Non-Fiction Books for Authors

How to Write a Novel

How to Write Non-Fiction

How to Make a Living with your Writing

Your Author Business Plan

How to Market a Book

The Successful Author Mindset

Productivity for Authors

Successful Self-Publishing

The Relaxed Author

Public Speaking for Authors, Creatives and Other Introverts

Audio for Authors: Audiobooks, Podcasting, and Voice Technologies

The Healthy Writer

Business for Authors

Co-writing a Book

Career Change

Artificial Intelligence, Blockchain, and Virtual Worlds

You can also find my Courses for Authors at:

www.TheCreativePenn.com/courses

Fiction as J.F. Penn

You can find my books in all formats on your favourite online store. You can also buy them direct from me at:

www.JFPennBooks.com

ARKANE Action-adventure Thrillers

Stone of Fire #1
Crypt of Bone #2
Ark of Blood #3
One Day In Budapest #4
Day of the Vikings #5
Gates of Hell #6
One Day in New York #7
Destroyer of Worlds #8
End of Days #9
Valley of Dry Bones #10
Tree of Life #11
Tomb of Relics #12

Brooke and Daniel Crime Thrillers

Desecration #1
Delirium #2
Deviance #3

Mapwalker Dark Fantasy Trilogy

Map of Shadows #1
Map of Plagues #2
Map of the Impossible #3

Other Books and Short Stories

Risen Gods

Catacomb

A Thousand Fiendish Angels: Short stories based on
Dante's Inferno

Soldiers of God

The Dark Queen:
An Underwater Archaeology Short Story

Blood, Sweat, and Flame

A Midwinter Sacrifice

More books coming soon.

You can sign up to be notified of new releases, giveaways
and pre-release specials - plus, get a free book!

www.JFPenn.com/free

About Joanna Penn

Joanna Penn writes non-fiction for authors and is an award-nominated, New York Times and USA Today best-selling thriller author as J.F. Penn.

She's also an award-winning podcaster, creative entrepreneur, and international professional speaker. She lives in Bath, England with her husband and enjoys a nice G&T.

Joanna's award-winning site for writers, TheCreativePenn. com, helps people to write, publish and market their books through articles, audio, video and online products as well as live workshops.

Buy my books direct
www.CreativePennBooks.com

Love thrillers?
www.jfpennbooks.com

Love travel? Check out my Books and Travel podcast
www.BooksAndTravel.page

www.TheCreativePenn.com
joanna@TheCreativePenn.com

www.twitter.com/thecreativepenn
www.facebook.com/TheCreativePenn
www.Instagram.com/jfpennauthor
www.youtube.com/thecreativepenn

Acknowledgements

Thank you to my community and patrons at The Creative Penn website and podcast. I hope this book helps you delve deeper into your writing craft.

Thanks especially to those who completed my Shadow Survey in the summer of 2023. Your words helped me in the final stages of the manuscript.

Thanks to fantastic horror author Michaelbrent Collings who has taught me much about the Shadow.

Thanks to Kristen Tate at The Blue Garret for brilliant editing and advice.

Thanks as ever to Jane Dixon Smith, JD Smith Design, for the cover design and print interior formatting.

And as always, thanks to Jonathan, who lets my dark horse run.

ND - #0028 - 180124 - C1 - 203/127/14 - PB - 9781915425416 - Matt Lamination